ASA Aeronautical Chart User's Guide

Aviation Supplies & Academics, Inc.

Aeronautical Chart User's Guide

Originally published by
National Oceanic and Atmospheric Administration,
U.S. Department of Commerce, 1991

Reprinted and published 1993 by
Aviation Supplies & Academics, Inc.
7005 132nd Place SE
Renton, Washington 98059-3153

ISBN 1-56027-192-2
ASA-CUG

Printed in Canada

99 98 97 96 95 94 93   9 8 7 6 5 4 3 2 1

INTRODUCTION

This Chart User's Guide is intended to serve as a learning aid, reference document and an introduction to the wealth of information provided on the aeronautical charts and publications of the National Oceanic and Atmospheric Administration (NOAA). This guide can also serve as a basic review of chart information for experienced pilots.

NOAA publishes charts for each stage of VFR (Visual Flight Rules) and IFR (Instrument Flight Rules) flight including planning, departure, enroute (low and high altitude), approach, and taxiing. Section 2 of this publication describes these charts and other aeronautical products. Chart coverage, ordering instructions, and a list of NOAA chart agents are included in the NOAA Aeronautical Chart Catalog, available free upon request from:

NOAA Distribution Branch, N/CG33
National Ocean Service
Riverdale, MD 20737-1199

Terms and abbreviations used in this publication are defined in the FAA (Federal Aviation Administration) Airman's Information Manual (AIM) Pilot/Controller Glossary. Unless otherwise indicated, miles are nautical miles, altitudes are in feet above Mean Sea Level (MSL), and times are Coordinated Universal Time (UTC).

To be assured of having the most current information, pilots should also refer to other sources, particularly those listed in this booklet under "Additional Publications for Pilots". Chart symbols in this guide are current to January, 1994.

USING CURRENT CHARTS

Use of obsolete charts or publications for navigation may be dangerous. Aeronautical information changes rapidly, and it is vitally important that pilots check the effective dates on each aeronautical chart and publication to be used. Obsolete charts and publications should be discarded and replaced by current editions.

To make certain a chart or publication is current, refer to the next scheduled edition date printed on the cover. Pilots should also consult Aeronautical Chart Bulletins in the **Airport/Facility Directory** and Notices to Airmen (NOTAMs) for changes essential to the safety of flight that may occur during the effective dates of a chart or publication.

Class II NOTAMs also include current Flight Data Center NOTAMs, which are regulatory in nature and primarily reflect changes to Standard Instrument Approach Procedures (SIAPs), flight restrictions, and aeronautical chart revisions. This publication is prepared every 14 days by the Federal Aviation Administration, and is available by subscription from the Government Printing Office.

REPORTING CHART DISCREPANCIES

Every effort is made to ensure that each piece of information shown on NOAA's charts and publications is accurate. Source materials are verified to the maximum extent possible.

You, the pilot, are perhaps NOAA's most valuable source of information. You are encouraged to notify NOAA, National Ocean Service, of any discrepancies you observe while using their charts and related publications. Postage-paid chart correction cards are available at FAA Flight Service Stations for this purpose (or you may write directly to NOAA, at the address below). Should delineation of data be required, mark and clearly explain the discrepancy on a current chart (a replacement copy will be returned to you promptly). Mail the corrected chart to the address below.

National Ocean Service
NOAA, N/CG31
6010 Executive Boulevard
Rockville, MD 20852

(Telephone Toll-Free 1-800-626-3677)

SECTION 1: EXPLANATION OF TERMS AND SYMBOLS

EXPLANATION OF VFR TERMS AND SYMBOLS

The discussions and examples in this section will be based on the Sectional Aeronautical Charts. These charts include the most current data and are at a scale most beneficial to pilots flying under visual flight rules. A pilot should have little difficulty in reading these charts which are, in many respects, similar to automobile road maps. Each chart is named for a major city within its area of coverage.

The chart legend lists various aeronautical symbols as well as information concerning terrain and contour elevations. You may identify aeronautical, topographical, and obstruction symbols (such as radio and television towers) by referring to the legend. Many landmarks which can be easily recognized from the air, such as stadiums, race tracks, pumping stations, and refineries, are identified by brief descriptions adjacent to small black squares marking their exact locations ▪ cabin . Oil wells are shown by small circles ₒ oil well . Water tanks and gas tanks are shown by small black circles ● water and labeled accordingly. The depictions of many items are exaggerated on the charts for improved legibility.

NOAA charts are prepared in accordance with specifications of the Interagency Air Cartographic Committee (IACC), and are approved by representatives of the Federal Aviation Administration, the Department of Commerce, and the Department of Defense. Some information on these charts may only apply to military pilots.

TERRAIN AND OBSTRUCTIONS

The elevation and configuration of the Earth's surface below are certainly of prime importance to pilots. Cartographers devote a great deal of attention to showing relief and obstruction data in a clear and concise manner. Five different techniques are used to show this information: Contour lines, shaded relief, color tints, obstruction symbols, and Maximum Elevation Figures.

1. Contour lines are lines connecting points on the Earth of equal elevation above mean sea level. On Sectional Aeronautical Charts, basic contours are spaced at 500-foot intervals. Intermediate con-  tours may also be shown at 250-foot intervals in moderately level or gently rolling areas. Occasionally, auxiliary contours at 50-, 100-, 125-, or 150-foot intervals may be used to portray smaller relief features in areas of relatively low relief. The pattern of these lines and their spacing gives the viewer a visual concept of the terrain. Widely spaced contours represent gentle slopes, while closely spaced contours represent steep slopes.

2. Shaded relief is a manual or computer-generated depiction of how the terrain might appear from the air. The cartographer shades the areas that would appear in shadow if illuminated by a light from the northwest. Studies have indicated that our visual perception has been  conditioned to this view.

3. Color tints are used to depict bands of elevation. These colors range from light green for the lowest elevations to brown for the higher elevations.

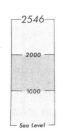

4. Obstruction symbols are used to depict man-made vertical features that may affect the national airspace. NOAA maintains a file of over 60,000 obstacles in the United States,

Canada, the Caribbean and Mexico. Each obstacle is verified by the cartographers before it is added to the visual charts. When the position or elevation of an obstacle is unverified, it is marked UC (under construction or reported).

The data in the obstruction file is collected and disseminated by the FAA as part of their responsibility for managing the National Airspace System under the Federal Aviation Regulations. Other data on licensed radio transmission towers is provided by the Federal Communications Commission.

Source data on terrain and obstructions is sometimes not complete or accurate enough for use in aeronautical publications; for example, a reported obstruction may be plotted on a map with insufficient detail for determining the obstruction's position and elevation. Such cases are investigated by the NOAA Flight Edit program.

Flight edit is conducted by NOAA Corps aviators in an aircraft equipped with an aerial mapping camera. The pilots visually verify cultural and topographic features and review all obstacle data.

This review includes checking for obstructions that may have been constructed, altered, or dismantled without proper notification. Unverified obstacles are photographed and the position and elevation are accurately determined photogrammetrically.

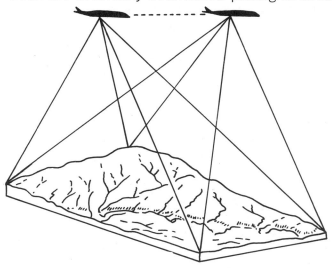

Generally, only man-made features extending more than 200 feet above ground level are charted. Objects 200 feet or less are charted only if they are considered obstructions, for example, if the location is much higher than the surrounding terrain or very near an airport. Examples of features considered obstacles to low level flight are antennae, tanks, factories, lookout towers, smokestacks, and elevated cables or pipelines crossing rivers or valleys.

Obstacles less than 1000 feet above ground level are shown by the symbol ∧ . Obstacles 1000′ and higher above ground level are shown by the symbol ⋏ . Manmade features which can be seen clearly from the air and can be used as checkpoints may be represented with pictorial symbols shown in black with the required elevation data in blue.

GOLDEN GATE BRIDGE

The height of the structure above ground level and the elevation of the top of the obstacle above sea level are shown when known or when they can be reliably determined by the cartographer. The height above ground level is shown in parentheses below the elevation above mean sea level of the top of the obstacle (650) . In extremely congested areas the above-ground-level values may be omitted to avoid confusion.

Obstacles are portrayed wherever possible. But since legibility would be impaired if all obstacles within city complexes or within high density groups of obstacles were portrayed, only the highest obstacle in an area is shown using ⋏ 2468 (1248) the group obstacle symbol.

Obstacles under construction are indicated by the letters UC immediately adjacent to the symbol. If available, the eventual above ground level height of the obstruction is shown in parentheses, for example, (1501) . Obstacles with high intensity strobe lighting systems are shown as ⋏ ⋇ .

5. The Maximum Elevation Figure (MEF) represents the highest elevation, including terrain and other vertical obstacles (towers, trees, etc.), bounded by ticked lines of graticule. Graticules on Sectional Aeronautical Charts are the lines dividing each 30 minutes of latitude and each 30 minutes of longitude. MEF figures are depicted to the nearest 100-foot value. The last two digits of

ATTENTION
THIS CHART CONTAINS MAXIMUM ELEVATION FIGURES (MEF). The Maximum Elevation Figures shown in quadrangles bounded by ticked lines of latitude and longitude are represented in THOUSANDS and HUNDREDS of feet above mean sea level. The MEF is based on information available concerning the highest known feature in each quadrangle, including terrain and obstructions (trees, towers, antennas, etc.).
12⁵
Example: 12,500 feet . . . .

the number are not shown. In the example the MEF represents 12,500 feet. MEFs are shown over land masses as well as over open water areas containing man-made obstacles such as oil rigs.

In the determination of MEFs, extreme care is exercised to increase such figures only to the minimum clearance altitude based on the existing elevation data shown on source material. Cartographers use the following procedure to calculate MEFs:

When a man-made obstacle is more than 200 feet above the highest terrain within the area bounded by ticked lines of graticule:

1. Determine the elevation of the top of the obstacle above mean sea level (MSL).
2. Add the possible vertical error of the source material to the above figure (100 feet or ½ contour interval when interval on source exceeds 200 feet. U.S. Geological Survey Quadrangle Maps with contour intervals as small as 10 feet are normally used).
3. Round the resultant figure up to the next higher hundred foot level.

Example: Elevation of obstacle top (MSL)= 2424
Possible vertical error   + 100
equals 2524
Raise to the following 100 foot level   2600

Maximum Elevation Figure (MSL) **2⁶**

When a natural terrain feature or natural vertical obstacle (e.g. a tree) is the highest feature within the area bounded by ticked lines of graticule:

1. Determine the elevation of the feature.
2. Add the possible vertical error of the source to the above figure (100 feet or ½ the contour interval when interval on source exceeds 200 feet).
3. Add a 200-foot allowance for natural or manmade obstacles which are not portrayed because they are below the minimum height at which the chart specifications require their portrayal.

4. Round the figure up to the next higher hundred foot level.

Example: Highest terrain elevation
(MSL)= 3450
Possible vertical error + 100
Allowance 200
equals 3750
Raise to the following 100 foot
level 3800
Maximum Elevation Figure (MSL) **38**

Pilots should be aware that while the MEF data are based on the best information available to the cartographer, the figures are not verified by field surveys. Also, you must consult the Aeronautical Chart Bulletin in the Airport/Facility Directory to ensure that your chart has the latest MEF data available.

RADIO AIDS TO NAVIGATION

On visual charts, information about radio aids to navigation is boxed, as illustrated. Duplication of data is avoided. When two or more radio aids in a general area have the same name with different frequencies, TACAN channel numbers, or identification letters, and no misinterpretation can result, the name of the radio aid may be indicated only once within the identification box. VHF/UHF radio aids to navigation names and identification boxes (shown in blue) take precedence. Only those items that are different (e.g., frequency, Morse Code) are repeated in the box in the appropriate color. The choice of separate or combined boxes is made in each case on the basis of economy of space and clear identification of the radio aids.

Radio aids to navigation located on an airport depicted by the pattern symbol may not always be shown by the appropriate symbol. Rather the type of radio aid to navigation may be indicated by letter identification; e.g., VOR, VORTAC, etc., positioned on and breaking the top line of the identification box.

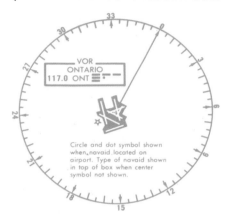

AIRPORTS

Airports in the following categories are charted as indicated (additional symbols are shown in Section 3 of this Chart User's Guide).

Public-use airports:

Hard-surfaced runways greater than 8000'

Hard-surfaced runways 1500' to 8000'

○ Other than hard-surfaced runways
⚓ Seaplane bases

Military airports:

◎ Other than hard-surfaced runways

Hard-surfaced runways are symbolized the same as public-use airports.

Military airports are identified by abbreviations such as AFB, NAS, AAF, NAAS, NAF, MCAS, or DND.

5

Services available:

Tick marks around the basic airport symbol indicate that fuel is available and the airport is tended during normal working hours.

Other airports with and without services: Ⓗ Ⓕ Ⓤ Ⓡ ⊗

Airports are plotted in their true geographic position unless the symbol conflicts with a radio aid to navigation (navaid) at the same location. In such cases, the airport symbol will be displaced, but the relationship between the airport and the navaid will be retained.

Airports are identified by their designated name. Military airport names all include abbreviations (such as AFB, NAS, AAF, NAAS, NAF, MCAS, or DND) indicating the type of facility. Generic parts of long airport names (such as "airport", "field", or "municipal") and the first names of persons are commonly omitted unless they are needed to distinguish one airport from another with a similar name.

The following figure illustrates the coded data that is provided along with the airport name. The elevation of an airport is the highest point on the useable portion of the landing areas. Runway length is the length of the longest active runway including displaced thresholds, and excluding overruns. Runway length is shown to the nearest 100 feet, using 70 as the division point; a runway 8070' long is charted as 81, and a runway 8069' long is charted as 80.

Airports with control towers, and their related information, are shown in blue. All other airports and their related information are shown in magenta (reddish purple).

The symbol ★ pertains to rotating or flashing airport beacons. The color or color combination displayed by a particular beacon and/or its auxiliary lights indicates whether the beacon identifies a landing place, landmark, or hazard. The symbol "L" indicates that runway lights are on during hours of darkness. The *L indicates that the pilot must consult another source (e.g., the Airport/Facility Directory) to determine the action necessary to turn on the runway lights. The lighted runway may not be the longest runway available, and may not be lighted full length. A detailed description of airport and air navigation lighting aids available at each airport can be found in the Airport/Facility Directory. The Airman's Information Manual thoroughly explains the types and uses of airport lighting aids.

CONTROLLED AIRSPACE

Controlled airspace consists of those areas where some or all aircraft may be subject to air traffic control, such as Class A, Class B, Class C, Class D, and Class E airspace.

The lateral and vertical limits of all controlled airspace, up to but not including 18,000 feet, are shown by narrow bands of vignette on Sectional Aeronautical Charts and Terminal Area Charts. Class E airspace is indicated with a magenta vignette, indicating a 700' AGL floor. Where the outer edge of the 700 foot transition area (magenta vignette) ends, the 1200 foot or greater area, automatically begins. With floors 1200' or greater above the surface, a light-blue shaded vignette line is used, indicating Class G, or uncontrolled, airspace.

Class E Airspace with floor 700 ft. above surface

Class E Airspace with floor 1200 ft. or greater above surface that abuts Class G Airspace.

With floors other than 700 feet or 1200 feet, a light-blue shaded, staggered, vignette line is used with the ceiling indicated above the line, and the floor indicated below the line   2400 MSL / 4500 MSL

Class D and Class E airspace, in which there are instrument approaches, are shown in their entirety and are depicted at their true geographic position regardless of the necessity to offset the airport symbol.

CLASS D AIRSPACE

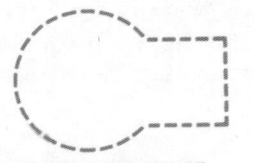

CLASS E AIRSPACE

Rotating Beacon
Airport Surveillance Radar
Non-Federal
Control Tower
Automatic Terminal Information Service
Elevation
Lighting
Length
Longest Runway
Visual Flight Rules Advisory Service

Ⓡ FSS FLUSHING (FLU)
NFCT - 123.2★ Ⓒ
ATIS 126.65
81 L 98 122.95
VFR Advsy 120.2
Airport of entry

Indicates Flight Service Station on field
Name in Airport Box indicates Special Traffic Area (see FAR 93)
Location Identifier
Common Traffic Advisory Frequency (CTAF)
Primary Local Control Frequency Star indicates non-continuous tower operation
ATIS Frequency
Unicom Frequency "U" only on WAC

Special VFR is only identified at airports where it is not **allowed.** It is depicted by a "NO SVFR" statement above the airport box

Class B Airspace is shown in abbreviated forms on World Aeronautical Charts and on Sectional Aeronautical Charts. Terminal Area Charts show Class B airspace in greater detail. Each sector is labeled with its delimiting altitudes, radials, and arcs. Air Traffic Control frequencies are also prominently shown on the Terminal Area Charts. The reverse of the chart shows the detailed rules and requirements associated with the particular Class B airspace.

Class C Airspace is symbolized by a solid magenta outline of the entire area and the sector within the area:▬▬▬ Class C Airspace (Mode C See F.A.R. 91.215/AIM.)

The MSL ceiling and floor altitudes of each sector are shown in solid magenta figures with the last two digits eliminated: $\frac{45}{17}$

The name by which the Class C airspace is identified is shown as follows:

Baltimore Class C

Separate notes, enclosed in magenta boxes, give the approach control frequencies to be used by arriving VFR aircraft to establish two-way radio communication before entering the Class C airspace (generally 20 NM):

ARRIVING VFR AIRCRAFT SHOULD CONTACT BOISE APPROACH CONTROL WITHIN 20 NM ON 119.6 269.4

SPECIAL USE AIRSPACE

Special use airspace confines certain flight activities and restricts entry, or cautions other aircraft operating within specific boundaries. Except for Controlled Firing Areas, special use airspace areas are depicted on visual aeronautical charts. Controlled Firing Areas are not charted because their activities are suspended immediately when spotter aircraft, radar, or ground lookout positions indicate an aircraft might be approaching the area. So nonparticipating aircraft are not required to change their flight paths. Special use airspace areas are shown in their entirety (within the limits of the chart), even when they overlap,

adjoin, or when an area is designated within another area. The areas are identified by type and identifying name or number, positioned either within or immediately adjacent to the area.

PROHIBITED, RESTRICTED OR WARNING AREA

P-56 OR R-6401 OR W-518

ALERT AREA

A-631 CONCENTRATED STUDENT HELICOPTER TRAINING

VANCE 2 MOA

OTHER AIRSPACE AREAS

Mode C Required Airspace (from the surface to 10,000' MSL) within 30 NM radius of the primary airport(s) for which a Class B airspace is designated, is depicted by a solid blue line, when it is not otherwise shown (i.e., by a Class B 30 NM arc around primary airport). Mode C is also depicted within 10 NM of any airport listed in Appendix D of FAR 91.215. Mode C is required by not depicted for operations within and above all Class C airspace up to 10,000' MSL. Enroute Mode C requirements (at and above 10,000' MSL except in airspace at and below 2,500 ft AGL) are not depicted. See FAR 91.215 and the Airman's Information Manual (AIM).

▬▬▬ MODE C (See F.A.R. 91.215/AIM.)

Class D Airspace are indicated on VFR charts by a broken, blue line around the associated airport.

- - - - Class D Airspace/Canadian Class C or F Control Zone

National Security Areas are indicated on the VFR charts with a broken magenta line. Unauthorized aircraft are requested to remain clear of these areas.

▬▬ ▬▬ National Security Area

Terminal Radar Service Areas (TRSAs) are shown in their entirety, symbolized by a black outline of the entire area including the various sectors within the area.

Most TRSAs are found associated within a Class D airspace, which would be depicted by a blue segmented line inside of the black outline.

■■■■■■ Terminal Radar Service
        Area (TRSA)

Military Training Routes (MTRs) are shown on Sectional and Terminal Area Charts and are identified by the route designator, e.g., ~~~~~~ IR147 ~ ~~~~~~ . Route designators are shown in solid black on the route centerline, positioned along the route for continuity. The designator IR or VR is not repeated when two or more routes are established over the same airspace, e.g., IR201-205-227. Routes numbered 001 to 099 are shown as IR1 or VR99, eliminating the initial zeros. Direction of flight along the route is indicated by small arrowheads adjacent to and in conjunction with each route designator.

The following note appears on the front panel of all Sectional Aeronautical Charts and on the upper right hand panel of VFR Terminal Area Charts covering the conterminous United States.

```
┌──────── MILITARY TRAINING ROUTES (MTRs) ────────┐
│ All IR and VR MTRs are shown, and may extend from the surface upwards. Only │
│ the route centerline, direction of flight along the route and the route designator │
│ are depicted – route widths and altitudes are not shown. │
│                                                                              │
│ Since these routes are subject to change every 56 days, and the charts are │
│ reissued every 6 months, you are cautioned and advised to contact the nearest │
│ FSS for route dimensions and current status for those routes affecting your │
│ flight. │
│                                                                              │
│ Routes with a change in the alignment of the charted route centerline will be │
│ indicated in the Aeronautical Chart Bulletin of the Airport/Facility Directory. │
│ Also, the VFR Wall Planning Chart is issued every 56 days and displays current │
│ route configurations and a composite tabulation of altitudes along these routes. │
│                                                                              │
│ Military Pilots refer to Area Planning AP/1B Military Training Routes North and │
│ South America for current routes. │
└──────────────────────────────────────────────────┘
```

There are IFR (IR) and VFR (VR) routes as follows:
Route identification:
(a) Routes at or below 1,500 feet AGL (with no segment above 1,500 feet) are identified by four-digit numbers; e.g., VR1007, etc. These routes are generally developed for flight under visual flight rules.
(b) Routes above 1,500 feet AGL (segments of these routes may be below 1,500 feet) are identified by three-digit or less numbers; e.g., IR008, VR058, etc. These routes are developed for flight under instrument flight rules

Route widths vary for each MTR and can extend several miles on either side of the charted MTR centerline. Detailed route width information is available in the Flight Information Publication (FLIP) AP/1B (a Department of Defense publication), or in the Digital Aeronautical Chart Supplement (DACS).

Special Military Activity areas are indicated on the Sectional Charts by a boxed note in black type. The note contains radio frequency information for obtaining area activity status.

```
┌────── SPECIAL MILITARY ACTIVITY ──────┐
│ CONTACT EDWARDS APPROACH CONTROL ON 133.65 │
│           FOR ACTIVITY STATUS │
└──────────────────────────────────────┘
```

TERMINAL AREA CHART (TAC) COVERAGE

Terminal Area Chart coverage is shown on appropriate Sectional Charts by a ¼″ screened blue line as indicated below. Within this area, pilots should use TAC's which provide greater detail and clarity of information. A note to this effect appears near the blue boundary line.

```
┌────────── LAS VEGAS TERMINAL AREA ──────────┐
│ Pilots are encourged to use the Las Vegas VFR Terminal Area Chart │
│ for flight at and below 9000′. Terminal Area Chart provide greater │
│ detail and clarify of information in congested terminal areas. │
└──────────────────────────────────────────────┘
```

EXPLANATION OF IFR TERMS AND SYMBOLS

The discussions and examples in this section will be based primarily on the IFR (Instrument Flight Rule) Enroute Low Altitude charts. Other IFR products use similar symbols in various colors (see Section 5 of this guide). The chart legends list aeronautical symbols with a brief description of what each symbol depicts. This section will provide a more detailed discussion of some of the symbols and how they are used on IFR charts.

NOAA charts are prepared in accordance with specifications of the Interagency Air Cartographic Committee (IACC), which are approved by representatives of the Federal Aviation Administration, the Department of Commerce, and the Department of Defense. Some information on these charts may only apply to military pilots.

AIRPORTS

All active airports with hard-surfaced runways of 3000' or longer are shown on NOAA IFR Enroute charts. All active airports with approved instrument approach procedures are also shown regardless of runway length or composition. Charted airports are classified according to the following criteria:

Airports and seaplane bases with an approved Low Altitude Instrument Approach Procedure published in the NOAA TPP (Terminal Procedures Publication) volumes.

Airports with an approved Department of Defense (DOD) Low Altitude Instrument Approach Procedure and/or DOD RADAR MINIMA published in DOD FLIPs (Flight Information Publications), the Supplement Alaska or the Terminal Alaska volume.

Airports and seaplane bases that do not have a published Instrument Approach Procedure.

Airports are plotted in their true geographic position unless the symbol conflicts with a radio aid to navigation (navaid) at the same location. In such cases, the airport symbol will be displaced, but the relationship between the airport and the navaid is retained.

Airports are identified by the airport name. In the case of military airports, the abbreviated letters AFB (Air Force Base), NAS (Naval Air Station), NAF (Naval Air Field), MCAS (Marine Corps Air Station), AAF (Army Air Field), etc., appear as part of the airport name.

Airports marked "Pvt" immediately following the airport name are not for public use, but otherwise meet the criteria for charting as specified above.

Runway length is the length of the longest active runway (including displaced thresholds but excluding overruns) and is shown to the nearest 100 feet using 70 feet as the division point; e.g., a runway of 8,070' is labeled 81.

The following runway compositions (materials) constitute a hard-surfaced runway: asphalt, bitumen, concrete, and tar macadam. Runways that are not hard-surfaced have a small letter "s" following the runway length, indicating a soft surface.

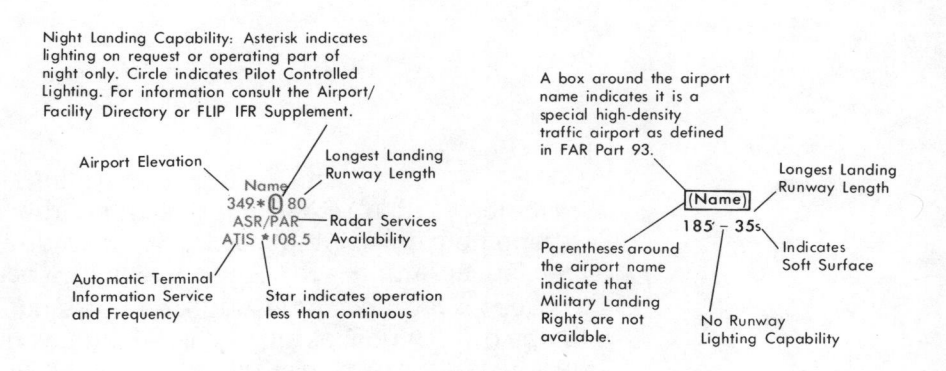

An "L" following the elevation under the airport name means that runway lights are on during hours of darkness. A circle around the "L" indicates there is Pilot Controlled Lighting. An asterisk beside the "L" means the lighting is less than continuous. The pilot should consult the Airport/Facility Directory for light operating procedures. The Airman's Information Manual thoroughly explains the types and uses of airport lighting aids.

RADIO AIDS TO NAVIGATION (NAVAIDS): All IFR radio navaids that have been flight-checked and are operational are shown on IFR enroute charts. VHF/UHF navaids (VORs, TACANs, and UHF NDBs) are shown in blue or black, and L/MF navaids (Compass Locators and Aeronautical or Marine NDBs) are shown in brown.

On enroute charts, information about radio navaids is boxed as illustrated below. To avoid duplication of data, when two or more radio navaids in a general area have the same name, the name is usually printed only once inside an identification box with the frequencies, TACAN channel numbers, identification letters, or Morse Code identifications of the different navaids all shown in appropriate colors. The decision to use separate or combined boxes is made in each case on the basis of reducing chart clutter and providing clear identification of the radio navaids.

In extremely congested areas, the navaid box will contain only the 3-letter identifier, and you will find the complete navaid box in the nearest open area on the chart.

Radio navaids that may be scheduled for some alteration within the lifespan of the charts have an operational note added. This operational note includes the projected dates and new frequency, when known, and advises the pilot of the contemplated action. The affected component is indicated by diagonal lines over the frequency or channel.

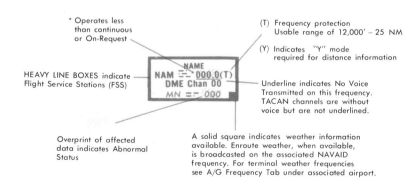

* Operates less than continuous or On-Request

(T) Frequency protection Usable range of 12,000' – 25 NM

(Y) Indicates "Y" mode required for distance information

HEAVY LINE BOXES indicate Flight Service Stations (FSS)

Underline indicates No Voice Transmitted on this frequency. TACAN channels are without voice but are not underlined.

Overprint of affected data indicates Abnormal Status

A solid square indicates weather information available. Enroute weather, when available, is broadcasted on the associated NAVAID frequency. For terminal weather frequencies see A/G Frequency Tab under associated airport.

CONTROLLED AIRSPACE: Controlled airspace consists of those areas where some or all aircraft may be subjected to air traffic control, such Class A, Class B, Class C, Class D, and Class E airspace.

All controlled airspace (Class E) on Enroute Low Altitude Charts, including transition area and additional control areas, up to, but not including 14,500' MSL are shown as open areas (white). Uncontrolled airspace (Class G) up to, but not including 14,500' MSL is shown as a brown shaded area. Control area extensions are depicted on the chart to their true scale and are shown as open area (white).

Class D and Class E airspace, in which there are instrument approaches, are shown in their entirety and are depicted at their true geographic position regardless of the need to offset the airport symbol. This airspace within the area of coverage of an Area Chart are shown on the Area Chart and are not shown on the Enroute Low Altitude Chart.

Airspace within which fixed-wing special VFR flight is prohibited is identified by a "SVFR" statement above the airport box.

Terminal Control Areas (TCAs) and Airport Radar Service Areas (ARSAs) consist of controlled airspace extending upward from the surface or a designated floor to specified altitudes, within which all aircraft and pilots are subject to the operating rules and requirements specified in the Federal Aviation Regulations (FAR) 71. TCAs and ARSAs are shown in abbreviated forms on Enroute Low Altitude Charts, and their limits are shown by a light blue tint and a thin blue outline. A general note adjacent to the TCA states the maximum elevation of the TCA. This note also refers the user to the appropriate VFR Terminal Area Chart.

Air Route Traffic Control Centers (ARTCC) are established to provide Air Traffic Control to aircraft operating on IFR flight plans within controlled airspace, particularly during the enroute phase of flight. Boundaries of the ARTCCs are shown in their entirety using the symbol below. Center names are shown adjacent and parallel to the boundary line.

MEMPHIS
~~~~~~
ATLANTA

ARTCC sector frequencies are shown in boxes outlined by the same symbol.

ARTCC Remoted Sites

SPECIAL USE AIRSPACE: Special use airspace confines certain flight activities or restricts entry, or cautions other aircraft operating within specific boundaries. Except for Controlled Firing Areas, special use airspace areas are depicted on aeronautical charts. Special use airspace areas are shown in their entirety, even when they overlap, adjoin, or when an area is designated within another area. The areas are identified by type and identifying number or name (R-4001), effective altitudes, operating time, weather conditions (VFR/IFR) during which the area is in operation, and voice call of the controlling agency; this information is positioned within or immediately adjacent to the area. Special Use Airspace with a floor of 18,000' MSL or above is not shown on the Enroute Low Altitude Charts. Similarly, Special Use Airspace with a ceiling below 18,000' MSL is not shown on Enroute High Altitude Charts.

CAMPBELL 1 MOA
500 AGL TO 10000
INTERMITTENT
1300-0200Z‡ MON-SUN
OTHER TIMES BY NOTAM
MEMPHIS CENTER/FSS

OTHER AIRSPACE:

Mode C Required Airspace (from the surface to 10,000' MSL) within 30 NM radius of the primary airport(s) for which Class B airspace is designated, is depicted on Enroute Low Altitude Charts. Mode C is also depicted within 10 NM of all airports listed in Appendix D of FAR 91.215 and the Airman's Information Manual (AIM).

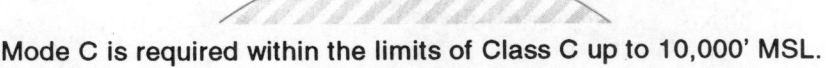

Mode C is required within the limits of Class C up to 10,000' MSL.

INSTRUMENT AIRWAYS

The FAA has established two fixed route systems for air navigation. The VOR and L/MF (low or medium frequency) system—designated from 1,200' AGL to but not including 18,000' MSL—is shown on Low Altitude Enroute Charts, and the Jet Route system—designated from 18,000' MSL to FL 450 inclusive—is shown on High Altitude Enroute Charts.

VOR L/MF AIRWAY SYSTEM
(LOW ALTITUDE ENROUTE CHARTS)

In this system VOR airways—airways based on VOR or VORTAC navaids—are depicted in blue and identified by a "V" (Victor) followed by the route number (e.g., "V12"). In Alaska, some segments of low-altitude airways are based on L/MF navaids and are charted in brown instead of blue.

L/MF airways—airways based on L/MF navaids—are sometimes called "colored airways" because they are identified by color name and number (e.g., "Amber One", charted as "A-1"). Green and Red airways are plotted east and west, and Amber and Blue airways are plotted north and south. Regardless of their color identifier, L/MF airways are shown in brown. U.S. colored airways exist only in Alaska; those within the conterminous U.S. have been rescinded.
(Note: In Mexican airspace on NOAA charts, L/MF airways are charted in blue.)

JET ROUTE SYSTEM
(HIGH ALTITUDE ENROUTE CHARTS)

Jet routes are based on VOR or VORTAC navaids, and are depicted in black with a "J" identifier followed by the route number (e.g., "J12"). In Alaska, some segments of jet routes are based on L/MF navaids and are shown in brown instead of black.

AIRWAY/ROUTE DATA

On both series of Enroute Charts, airway/route data such as the airway identifications, bearings or radials, mileages, and altitude (e.g., MEA, MOCA, MAA) are shown aligned with the airway and in the same color as the airway.

Airways/Routes predicated on VOR or VORTAC navaids are defined by the outbound radial from the navaid. Airways/Routes predicated on L/MF navaids are defined by the inbound bearing.

MILITARY TRAINING ROUTES (MTRs):

Military Training Routes (MTRs) are routes established for the conduct of low-altitude, high-speed military flight training (generally below 10,000 feet MSL at airspeeds in excess of 250 knots IAS). These routes are depicted in brown ink on Enroute Low Altitude Charts, and are not shown on inset charts or on IFR Enroute High Altitude Charts. Enroute Low Altitude Charts depict all IR (IFR Military Training Route) and VR (VFR Military Training Route) routes, except those VRs that are entirely at or below 1500 feet AGL.

Military Training Routes are identified by designators (IR-107, VR-134) which are shown in brown on the route centerline. Arrows indicate the direction of flight along the route. The width of the route determines the width of the line that is plotted on the chart:

Route segments with a width of 5 NM or less, either side of the centerline, are shown by a .02" line.   IR-107➔ VR-134➔

Route segments with a width greater than 5 NM, either side of the centerline, are shown by a .035" line. IR-113➔ VR-133➔

SECTION 2: LISTING OF NOAA AERONAUTICAL PRODUCTS

PLANNING (VFR & IFR) CHARTS, PUBLICATIONS, AND FILES

VFR/IFR WALL PLANNING CHART

Scale: 1:2,333,232
      (1″=32 NM)
Size: 56″ x 82″ (Available
      Unfolded or Folded to
      8½″ x 14″)
Revision cycle: 56 days

This large chart is produced in two halves (East and West) which may be assembled to form a Low Altitude IFR planning chart on one side, and a VFR planning chart on the other. Coverage includes the continental U.S. and the Gulf of Mexico. Features shown on this chart include:

      ○ Low altitude airways
      ○ Mileages
      ○ Radio aids to navigation
      ○ Airports
      ○ Special use airspace
      ○ State boundaries
      ○ Large bodies of water
      ○ Time zones

The VFR Planning Chart also includes:

      ○ Military Training Routes
      ○ Military Refueling Tracks
      ○ Shaded relief & terrain elevations
      ○ Index of Sectional Charts

The Low Altitude IFR Planning Chart also includes:

      ○ Air Route Traffic Control Center (ARTCC) boundaries
      ○ Index of Enroute Low Altitude – U.S. Charts

FLIGHT CASE PLANNING CHART

Scale: 1:4,374,803
      (1″=60 NM)
Size: 30″ x 50″ (Folded to
      5″ x 10″)
Revision cycle: 24 weeks

This is a small-scale planning chart that is designed to be used for preflight and inflight planning of flights below 18,000′ MSL. Features shown on this chart include:

      ○ All features shown on the IFR Wall Planning Chart
      ○ Shaded relief and critical elevations
      ○ Selected Flight Service Stations (FSS)
      ○ Parachute Jumping Areas
      ○ Special Use Airspace Table
      ○ Mileage Table (distances between 174 major airports)
      ○ City/Airport Location Index (Lists all airports shown on the planning chart. Airports with Instrument Approach Procedures are identified by a "P", airports with National Weather Service offices are identified by a "W", and airports open to the public with NOTAM service, with the airport identifier immediately following the airport name.)
      ○ Indexes for Sectionals, Canadian, Pacific, and South American charts.
      ○ Time zones

OCEANIC ROUTE CHARTS

Oceanic Route Charts are designed for air traffic controllers to use in monitoring and coordination of oceanic flights. They may also be used by pilots for flight planning.

NORTH ATLANTIC ROUTE CHART

FULL SIZE
Scale: 1:5,500,000
        (1"=75 NM)
Size: 58" x 41" (Unfolded)

HALF SIZE
Scale: 1:11,000,000
        (1"=151 NM)
Size: 29" x 20½" (Folded
        to 5" x 10")
Revision cycle: 24 weeks

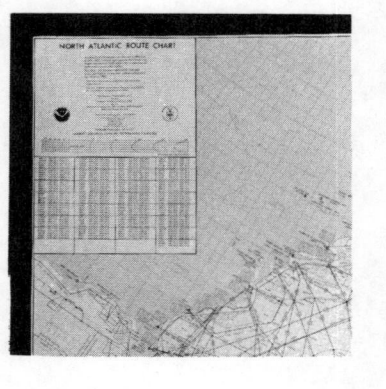

NORTH PACIFIC ROUTE CHARTS

COMPOSITE
Scale: 1:12,000,000
        (1"=165 NM)
Size: 59½" x 42½"
        (Unfolded)
Revision cycle: 56 days

AREA CHARTS
Scale: 1:7,000,000 (1"=96 NM)
Size: 59½" x 42½"
Revision cycle: 56 days

Features shown on these charts include:
- ATS Routes (Selected)
- Oceanic control areas
- NAVAIDS and reporting points (with geographic coordinates)
- NAT/MNPS (North Atlantic/Minimum Navigation Performance Specifications) area
- ADIZ (Air Defense Identification Zone)
- Airports of entry
- FIR (Flight Information Region) boundaries
- International boundaries
- Special use airspace

Features shown on these charts include:
- ATS Routes (Selected)
- NAVAIDS and reporting points (with geographic coordinates)
- International boundaries
- Buffer zones and non-free-flying areas
- ADIZ (Air Defense Identification Zone)
- International Date Line
- Aerial Refueling Tracks
- Special use airspace
- Airports of entry
- Mileage circles
- Oceanic control areas
- FIR (Flight Information Region) boundaries

DIGITAL AERONAUTICAL CHART SUPPLEMENT

Format:
PAPER COPY: (8½" x 11" booklets)
MAGNETIC TAPE: (9-track, 1600 bpi,
½" ASCII) (Sections 1-8)
Revision cycle: 56 days
(Section 9: 1-year cycle)

The individual sections are:

Section 1: High Altitude Airways – Conterminous U.S.
Section 2: Low Altitude Airways – Conterminous U.S.
Section 3: Selected Instrument Approach Procedure
NAVAID and Fix Data (Includes a 28-day
Change Notice)
Section 4: Military Training Routes
Section 5: Alaska, Hawaii, Puerto Rico, Bahama and
Selected Oceanic Routes
Section 6: STARs – Standard Terminal Arrivals and
Profile Descent Procedures
Section 7: SIDs – Standard Instrument Departures
Section 8: Preferred IFR Routes (Low and High Altitudes)
Section 9: Air Route and Airport Surveillance Radar
Facilities

The Digital Aeronautical Chart Supplement is specifically designed to provide digital airspace data not otherwise readily available. The supplement is produced every 56 days, except section 9 which is produced annually. Section 9 is not available in a digital format. Included with Section 3 is a *Change Notice* that is issued at the mid 28-day point containing changes that occurred after the 56-day publication.

Features provided in the DACS include:

○ Routes listed numerically by official designation
○ NAVAIDs & Fixes listed by official location identifier
○ Fixes without official location identifiers (airway intersections, ARTCC boundary crossing points) listed by 5-digit FAA computer code
○ Latitude & longitude for each fix listed to tenths of seconds
○ Magnetic variations at NAVAIDS
○ Controlling ARTCC
○ Military Training Route descriptions (scheduling activity, altitude data, & route width)
○ Preferred IFR Routes (include departure or arrival airport name, and effective times)
○ Radar facilities (ground elevation, radar tower height & type of radar facility)
○ Data which is new or deleted since the last edition is clearly marked or listed

NAVAID DIGITAL DATA FILE

Format
PAPER COPY:
(8½″ x 11″ computer hardcopy)
DISKETTE: (5¼″, 1.2 MB, MS-DOS,
ASCII)
MAGNETIC TAPE: (9-track, 1600 bpi,
½″ ASCII or EBCDIC)
Revision cycle: 56 days

This file contains the geographic position, type, and unique identifier for every navigational aid in the United States, Puerto Rico, and the Virgin Islands. These data are chart-independent, so can be applied to any NOS chart for which the data are required. Loran and RNAV avionics can use these data without modification. The data is government certified, and is compatible with the Air Route Traffic Control Center (ARTCC) system.

The information in this file is being made available in response to requests from the public, including avionics manufacturers, software developers, flight planning services, pilots, navigators, and other chart producers.

Data in the NAVAID file includes:

- ○NAVAID identifier
- ○Type NAVAID
- ○NAVAID status (commisioned or not commissioned)
- ○Latitude and longitude to tenths of seconds
- ○Name of NAVAID
- ○NAVAID service (high, low, terminal)
- ○Frequency of NAVAID, and channel where applicable
- ○NAVAID elevation
- ○Magnetic variation of record at the FAA
- ○ARTCC code where NAVAID is located
- ○State or country in which the NAVAID is located

OBSTRUCTION DATA SHEET (ODS)

Format: Paper copy only (8½″ x 11″)
Revision cycle: Same as associated OC

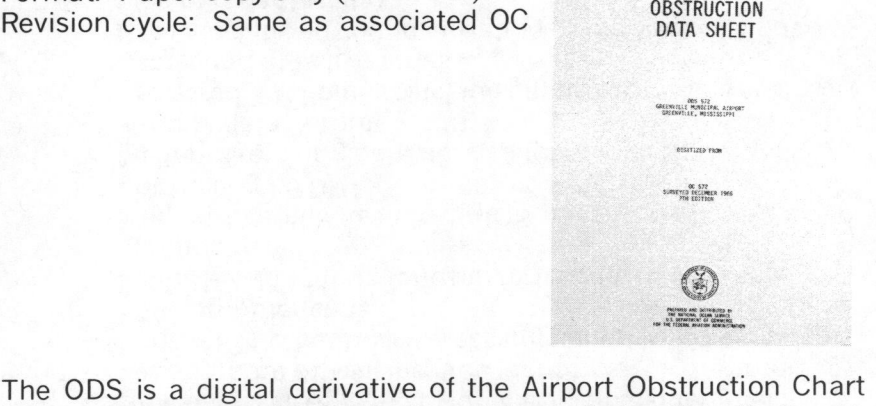

The ODS is a digital derivative of the Airport Obstruction Chart (OC). All objects, both obstructing and nonobstructing, that carry an elevation on the OC are listed in the ODS. Runway configuration and runway lengths, widths, and elevations are presented on the last page of the ODS.

DIGITAL OBSTACLE FILE

Format
PAPER COPY: (8½" x 11" hard copy)
MAGNETIC TAPE: (9-track, 1600 bpi,
½" ASCII or EBCDIC)
  Check on availability of Diskette & Tape
  from NOAA Distribution
Revision cycle: Quarterly
                Monthly

The quarterly file contains a complete listing of verified obstacles for the U.S., Puerto Rico, and the Virgin Islands with limited coverage of the Pacific, Caribbean, Canada and Mexico. Each obstacle is assigned a unique NOS numerical identifier. The obstacles are listed in ascending order of latitude within each state.

The monthly file contains all changes made to verified obstacles during the previous 4 week period. Both the old record (as it appeared before the change) and new record are shown.

Features of the file include:
  o Unique NOS obstacle identifier
  o Verification status
  o State
  o Associated city
  o Latitude and longitude (rounded to the nearest second)
  o Obstacle type
  o Number (if 2 or more)
  o Call sign and frequency (if charted)
  o Above ground level height
  o Above mean sea level height
  o Lighting (if known)
  o Accuracy code (both horizontal and vertical)
  o Marking (if known)
  o FAA study number
  o ''Last change'' code and Julian Date of that change

AIRPORT/FACILITY DIRECTORY

Format: Paper copy only
        (5 3/8" x 8¼"
        books)
Revision cycle: 56 days

This directory is an alphabetically listing of data on record with the FAA on all airports that are open to the public, associated terminal control facilities, ARTCCs, and radio aids to navigation within the conterminous U.S., Puerto Rico, and the Virgin Islands. Radio aids and airports are listed alphabetically. Airports and associated cities are cross-referenced. Features of this Directory include:

  o NOTAM service
  o Location identifier (used in flight plans)
  o Airport location (distance & direction from center of
    associated city)
  o Time conversion (time zone)
  o Geographic position of airport
  o Charts on which the facility is located
    (Sectional, Low & High Altitude Enroute and
    Instrument Approach Procedures)
  o Elevation
  o Rotating light beacon (if applicable)
  o Servicing available
  o Fuel available
  o Oxygen available
  o Traffic pattern altitude
  o Airport of Entry and Landing Rights Airports
  o Certified Airport (FAR 139 – availability of crash, fire,
    rescue equipment)
  o FAA inspection data

(continued on next page)

- Runway data (surface & length, weight bearing capacity, lighting, pilot-controlled airport lighting, visual glideslope indicators, runway gradient, displaced threshold and obstacle data)
- Airport remarks (landing fee, items affecting status & usability of airport)
- Weather data sources
- Communications
- Radio aids to navigation
- Bearing and distance from nearest usable VORTAC or VOR/DME facility.
- Detailed Directory Legend

SUPPLEMENT ALASKA

Format: Paper copy only
(5 3/8" x 8¼"
book)
Revision cycle: 56 days

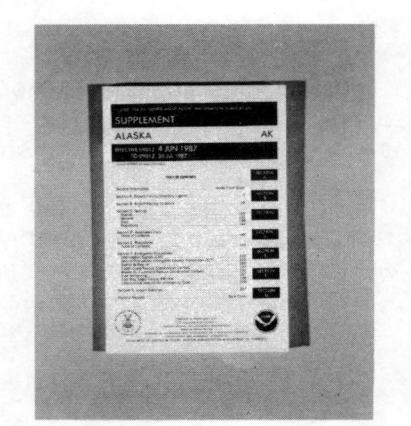

The Supplement is a joint civil-military Flight Information Publication (FLIP). It is designed for use with the Enroute Charts and the Terminal Alaska Publication covering Alaska and portions of Southwest and Northwest Canada. Features of this publication include:

- All of the features of the Airport/Facility Directory, including airports on Alaska Enroute charts.
- Notices (special, general, area, regulatory)
- Associated data (FAA HF/SSB Air-Ground Comm.

Stations, marine radio beacons, parachute jumping areas, Alaskan Forces Radio Network Stations, Standard Broadcast Stations, FSS & Special Reporting Service, Military Aerial Refueling, VFR Military Training Routes, Conversion tables)
- Special procedures (CIRVIS, MIJI, Cruising altitude diagrams, airport traffic light signals, Special VFR, ATC Radar Beacon System, Alaska ADIZ)
- Emergency procedures
- Airport sketches (for selected airports)
- Position reports format

AIRPORT OBSTRUCTION CHARTS (OC)

Scale: 1:12,000 (1" = 0.2 NM)
Format: 32" x 47" or 32" x 52"
(Folded to 6½" x 10")
Revision cycle: As required

These charts provide data for computing maximum take-off and landing weights of civil aircraft, for establishing instrument approach and landing procedures, and for engineering studies relative to obstruction clearing and improvements in airport facilities. Features shown on these charts include:

- Airport obstruction information
- FAR part 77 surfaces
- Runway plans and profiles
- Taxiways and ramp areas
- Air navigation facilities
- Selected planimetry
- An Obstruction Data Sheet (ODS) is provided at no additional cost with each OC.

GULF OF MEXICO AND CARIBBEAN PLANNING CHART

Scale: 1:6,192,178
      (1″ = 85 NM)
Size: 20″ x 34″
      (paper size is
      20″ x 60″ folded
      to 5″ x 10″)
Revision cycle: Annually

This one-color chart was designed to assist VFR pilots in planning their flights through and around the Gulf of Mexico and Caribbean Area. It is meant to be used in conjunction with World Aeronautical Charts, and is printed on the back of the Puerto Rico-Virgin Islands VFR Terminal Area Chart.

Features provided on this chart include:

- Airports of Entry
- Special Use Airspace effective below 18,000′ MSL, identified by ICAO location identifier, airspace prefix and number.
- Significant bodies of water
- International boundaries
- Large islands and island groups
- Capital cities and cities where an airport is located, selected other major cities
- Air mileages between Airports of Entry
- Index of World Aeronautical Charts
- Directory of Airports, including available facilities and servicing, and fuel octane
- Tabulation of U.S. Aeronautical Telecommunications Services for aircraft engaged in international or overseas flight (including Selective Calling System facilities)
- Partial list of U.S. government charts and publications for flights outside the U.S.
- Department of Defense requirements for civilian use of military fields
- Check-off list for ditching
- Runway Visual Range (RVR) conversion table (féet to meters)
- Emergency procedures (Flight outside U.S., pilot procedures, search and rescue, ground-air visual codes)

CHARTED VFR FLYWAY PLANNING CHART

Scale: 1:250,000
      (1″ = 3.43 NM)
Size: Same as the
      associated TAC
Revision cycle: Semiannually

These three-color charts are designed to assist pilots in planning flights through and/or around areas of high density aircraft operations such as Terminal Control Areas and Airport Radar Service Areas. The charts are designed to be used in conjunction with Sectional Aeronautical Charts and Terminal Area Charts (TACs), and are printed on the backs of selected TACs. The area of coverage of these charts is the same as the corresponding TACs.

These charts are for planning only and are not to be used for navigation.

Features of these charts include:

- Airports
- Navaids
- Special use airspace below 18,000′
- Terminal Control Areas and Airport Radar Service Areas
- Control Zones
- VFR flyways (bearings and altitudes)
- Procedural notes
- Military Training Routes
- Selected vertical obstacles
- VFR checkpoints
- Hydrographic features (bodies of water, drainage)
- Cultural features that lie beneath or adjacent to the VFR flyway, or that are designated VFR checkpoints (populated places, railroads, tanks, transmission lines, roads)
- Terrain relief that is designated as a VFR checkpoint, and critical spot elevations

VFR CHARTS AND PUBLICATIONS

SECTIONAL AERONAUTICAL CHARTS

Scale: 1:500,000
     (1" = 6.86 NM)
Size: 20" x 60" (Folded to
     5" x 10", 55 charts)
Revision cycle: Semiannually,
     except for some Alaskan
     charts which are
     revised annually

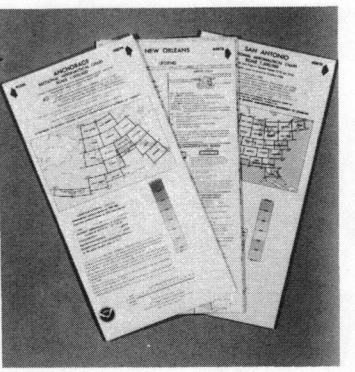

These multicolored charts are designed for visual navigation of slow to medium speed aircraft. Features shown on these charts include:

- Visual aids to navigation
- Radio aids to navigation
- Airports
- Common Traffic Advisory Frequencies
- Controlled airspace
- Restricted areas
- Obstructions
- Topography (including selected visual checkpoints such as populated places, drainage patterns, roads, railroads, and other distinctive landmarks)
- Shaded Relief
- Latitude and longitude lines
- Airways and fixes
- Other low level related data

TERMINAL AREA CHARTS

Scale: 1:250,000
     (1" = 3.43 NM)
Size: 20" x 25" (Folded to
     5" x 10", 23 charts)
Revision cycle: Semiannually

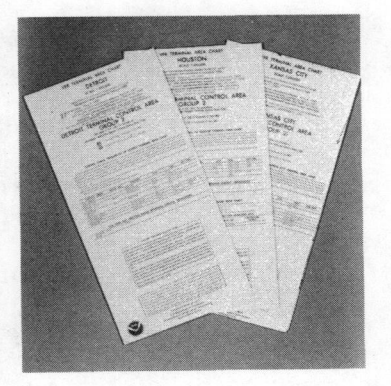

Multicolored Terminal Area Charts depict the airspace designated as Terminal Control Areas (TCAs). The information found on these charts, while similar to that found on Sectional Charts, is shown in much more detail on this larger scale chart. These charts are for the use of pilots operating from airfields within or near a Terminal Control Area. Locations of Terminal Area Charts are indicated on the Sectional Chart indicies. Features shown on these charts include:

- Visual aids to navigation
- Radio aids to navigation
- Airports
- Common Traffic Advisory Frequencies
- Controlled airspace
- Restricted areas
- Obstructions
- Topography
- Shaded Relief
- Latitude and longitude lines
- Airways and fixes
- Other low level related data

WORLD AERONAUTICAL CHARTS

Scale: 1:1,000,000
        (1″ = 13.7 NM)
Size: 20″ x 60″ (Folded to
        5″ x 10″, 27 charts)
Revision cycle: Annually,
        except for a few in
        Alaska and Central
        America which are
        revised bienially

World Aeronautical Charts cover land areas at a standard size and scale for navigation by moderate speed aircraft and aircraft operating at high altitudes. Because of their smaller scale these charts do not show as much detailed information as appears on the Sectional and Terminal Area Charts. For example, the limits of controlled airspace are not shown. Because some information is not shown, World Aeronautical Charts are not recommended for pilots of low speed, low altitude aircraft.

Features shown on these charts include:

○ Visual aids to navigation
○ Radio aids to navigation
○ Airports
○ Restricted areas
○ Obstructions
○ Topography (including city tints, principal roads, railroads distinctive landmarks, drainage patterns and relief)
○ Shaded Relief
○ Latitude and longitude lines
○ Airways
○ Other VFR-related data for medium speed aircraft

U.S. GULF COAST VFR AERONAUTICAL CHART

Scale: 1:1,000,000
         (1″ = 13.7 NM)
Size: 27″ x 55″ (Folded to
         5″ x 10″)
Revision cycle: Annually

This chart is designed primarily for helicopter operations in the Gulf of Mexico area. It is at the same scale as World Aeronautical Charts (WACs), and shows the same onshore features. Chart coverage extends south to 26°30′N.

Features shown on this chart in addition to those shown on WACs are:

○ Offshore mineral leasing areas and blocks
○ Oil drilling platforms
○ High density helicopter activity areas
○ Experimental Loran Offshore Flight Following (LOFF) routes

HELICOPTER ROUTE CHARTS

Scale: 1:125,000
       (1″ = 1.71 NM)
Size: 30″ x 30″ (Folded to
       5″ x 10″)
Revision cycle: As required

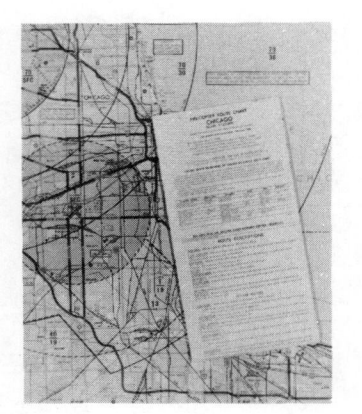

Available for: Boston, Chicago, Los Angeles, New York, and
                Baltimore-Washington *

These charts show principal helicopter routes in and around these cities. Other items depicted include:

- Pictorial symbols of prominent landmarks
- Public, private, and hospital heliports
- NAVAID and communications frequencies
- Common Traffic Advisory Frequencies
- Selected obstructions
- Roads
- Spot elevations
- Commercial broadcast stations
- TCA, ARSA, and Control Zone boundaries

The New York chart includes a larger scale inset of Lower Manhattan and the Hudson and East River.

*A Helicopter Route Chart for the Houston metropolitan area is scheduled for February 1992.

IFR CHARTS AND PUBLICATIONS

IFR ENROUTE HIGH ALTITUDE CHARTS

CONTERMINOUS U.S.
Scale: 1:2,187,402
      (1″ = 30 NM)

(H-6 scale is 1″=18 NM)
Size: 20″ x 55″ (Folded to
     5″ x 10″)

ALASKA
Scale: 1:3,281,102
      (1″ = 45 NM)
Size: 20″ x 50″ (Folded to
     5″ x 10″)

Revision cycle: 56 days

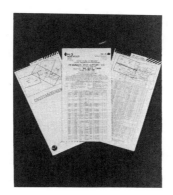

IFR Enroute High Altitude Charts are designed to provide navigation information for IFR flights at and above 18,000′ MSL. Some features of these charts include:

- Jet route structure (shown in black; non-enroute navaids are screened)
- Airspace information (shown in blue); Special Use Airspace is tabulated on the title panel
- Selected airports (all airports with at least 5000′ hard-surfaced runway, 4000′ on Alaska High H-1 & H-2). BLUE and GREEN Airports have an approved Instrument Approach Procedure published. The DOD FLIP Terminal High Altitude contains only those shown in BLUE. Brown – airports with no approved IAP
- VHF radio aids to navigation (frequency, ID, channel and geographic coordinates)
- Reporting points (geographic coordinates are provided for compulsory reporting points)

ENROUTE LOW ALTITUDE CHARTS

CONTERMINOUS U.S.
Scale: 1:583,307 (1″=8 NM) to
      1:1,458,267 (1″ = 20 NM)

ALASKA
Scale: 1:2,187,402
      (1″ = 30 NM)

AREA CHARTS
Scale: 1:364,567 (1″ = 5 NM) to
      1:583,307 (1″ = 8 NM)
Size: 20″ x .50″ (Folded to
     5″ x 10″)
Revision cycle: 56 days

Enroute Low Altitude Charts are designed to provide navigation information for IFR flights below 18,000′ MSL. Area Charts are larger-scale representations of congested terminal areas. Features shown on these charts include:

- Low altitude airways
- Limits of controlled airspace
- Radio aids to navigation (identification, & frequency)
- Selected airports
- Route altitude descriptions (MEAs, MOCAs, MCAs)
- Airway distances
- Reporting points
- Special use airspace
- Military Training Routes & related information
- Operational notes
- Adjoining chart numbers
- Outlines of Area Charts

U. S. TERMINAL PROCEDURES PUBLICATION (TPP)

INSTRUMENT APPROACH PROCEDURES (IAP)
STANDARD TERMINAL ARRIVALS (STAR)
STANDARD INSTRUMENT DEPARTURES (SID)
AIRPORT DIAGRAMS

Scale: IAP – Varied within volume
Usually 1:500,00 or
1:750,000
(individual charts to scale
except when concentric
rings shown)
STAR/SID – Charts generally
not to scale

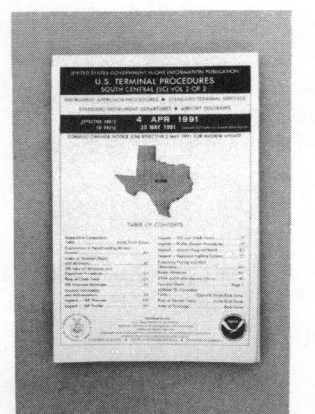

Format: Paper copy only
(5 3/8" x 8 1/4" bound books)

Revision cycle: 56 days

The TPP provides pilots with the charts required for landing, arrival, and departure published in 16 bound volumes covering the conterminous U.S. and the Puerto Rico-Virgin Islands.

The IAP charts portray the aeronautical data required to execute instrument approaches. Each procedure is designated for use with a specific navigational aid; e.g., ILS, MLS, VOR, NDB, LOC, LDA, SDF, LORAN.

STARs provide graphic and textual descriptions of pre-planned IFR air traffic control arrival procedures for pilot use. They reduce pilot/controller workload and air-ground communications, minimizing potental errors in delivery and receipt of clearances. Use of STARs also facilitates transition from the enroute environment to instrument approaches.

SIDs provide graphic and textual descriptions of standard instrument departure clearances. They are used to expedite clearance delivery and to facilitate transition between take-off and enroute operations.

Profile Descent Procedure Charts are also published in the TPP. A profile descent is an uninterrupted descent (except for level flight required for speed adjustment) from cruising altitude to the "approach gate" or interception of glide slope or other minimum altitude.

Features shown on these charts include:

o Related navigational data
o Communications frequencies
o Reporting points/fixes
o Transitional data
o Obstacles
o Drainage
o Minimum safe altitude
o Holding patterns
o Missed approach procedures
o Approach minima data
o Airport sketches
o Airport Lighting information
o Special use airspace
o Airways and mileages
o Changeover points
o Computer codes for filing flight plans
o Data for Inertial Navigation Systems

These TPP publications also include:

- Table of Contents
- IFR Takeoff Minimums and Departure Procedures
- IFR Alternate Minimums
- Rate-of-climb Table
- Inoperative Components Table
- Legend of Approach Lighting System
- Radar Minimums
- Explanation of Terms
- Planview Legend
- Profile Legend
- Airport Diagram/Sketch Legend
- Rate of Descent Table
- General Information and Abbreviations
- LORAN TD Correction Table

Airport Diagrams are specifically designed to assist in the movement of ground traffic at locations with complex runway/taxiway configurations and to provide information for Inertial Navigation Systems (INS).

CHART SUPPLEMENT PACIFIC

Format Paper copy only
        (5 3/8" x 8 1/4" book)
Revision cycle: 56 days
        (Amendment Notice published
        4 weeks after each issue)

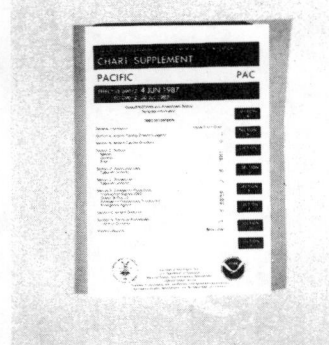

This supplement is designed for use with Flight Information Publication Enroute Charts and with the Sectional Aeronautical Chart covering the State of Hawaii and that area of the Pacific served by U.S. facilities. Features of this Supplement include:

- o Airport/Facility Directory of all "open to the public" airports and those requested by appropriate authority (See description of Airport/Facility Directory on Page 12.)
- o Communications data
- o Navigational facilities
- o Special notices
- o Special procedures
- o Instrument Approach Procedure Charts
- o Standard Instrument Departure Charts
- o Standard Terminal Arrival Charts
- o Airport diagrams
- o Radar minimums
- o IFR takeoff and departure procedures
- o IFR alternate minimums
- o Supplementary supporting data

TERMINAL ALASKA

Format Paper copy only
        (5 3/8" x 8 1/4" book)
Revision cycle: 56 days

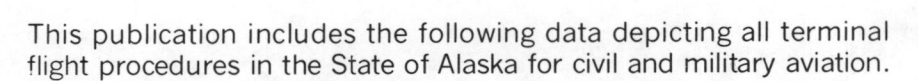

This publication includes the following data depicting all terminal flight procedures in the State of Alaska for civil and military aviation.

- o Instrument Approach Procedure (IAP) Charts
- o Standard Instrument Departure (SID) Charts
- o Standard Terminal Arrival (STAR) Charts
- o Airport Diagrams
- o Radar Minimums
- o IFR take-off and departure procedures
- o IFR alternate minimums
- o Rate of Descent Table
- o Inoperative Components Table
- o Selected planimetry
- o General information and abbreviations
- o IAP Legends for Planviews and Profiles
- o IAP Legends for Airport Diagrams/Airport Sketches
- o SID and STAR Legends
- o Rate of Climb Table

ADDITIONAL PUBLICATIONS FOR PILOTS

Additional sources of useful information for pilots are available from NOAA and other agencies. The following publications are suggested for both basic reference and supplementary data. For a complete list of available publications, please contact the individual agency at the address provided.

NATIONAL OCEANIC AND ATMOSPHERIC ADMINISTRATION

PUBLICATIONS AVAILABLE AT NO COST FROM NOAA

The following free publications are available upon request from:

NOAA Distribution Branch, N/CG33
National Ocean Service
Riverdale, MD 20737-1199
Phone: (301) 436-6990

NOAA CATALOG OF AERONAUTICAL CHARTS AND RELATED PRODUCTS

Revision Cycle: As required

Describes each IFR and VFR aeronautical chart and chart-related publication produced by NOAA, including digital products. Includes information about selected products available from the FAA. Lists chart agents, chart coverage, and other information needed to select and order charts and publications. Prices are contained in a separate annual Price List provided with the catalog.

NOAA SUBSCRIPTION ORDER BROCHURE FOR AERONAUTICAL CHARTS AND RELATED PRODUCTS

Revision Cycle: Annually

Contains complete ordering information and order forms for all NOAA aeronautical products available on a subscription basis.

FEDERAL AVIATION ADMINISTRATION

NOTICES TO AIRMEN

Revision Cycle: Biweekly

A publication containing current Notices to Airmen (NOTAMS) which are considered essential to the safety of flight as well as supplemental data affecting other operational publications. It also includes current Flight Data Center (FDC) NOTAMS, which are regulatory in nature, issued to establish restrictions to flight or to amend charts or published instrument approach procedures.

PILOT'S HANDBOOK OF AERONAUTICAL KNOWLEDGE

This handbook contains essential technical information used in training and guiding pilots. Subjects include the principles of flight, airplane performance, flight instruments, basic weather, navigation and charts, and excerpts from flight information publications.

* Available through your local ASA dealer.

GUIDE TO FEDERAL AVIATION ADMINISTRATION PUBLICATIONS

Revision Cycle: Annually

This sixty-page Guide contains information on the wide range of FAA documents and publications, and how they can be obtained. It lists available publications by category and gives the various sources. Listed also are civil aviation-related publications issued by other Federal agencies.

For a free copy, please order FAA-APA-PG-13 from:

U.S. Department of Transportation
M-443.2
Washington, D.C. 20590

The following FAA publication is available through the Government Printing Office, whose address is listed on the next page.

AIRMAN'S INFORMATION MANUAL (AIM)

Revision Cycle: 112 days

This manual contains fundamental procedural information required for safe flight in the U.S. National Airspace System. It includes chapters on navigation aids, airspace, air traffic control, flight safety, and safe operating practices. It also includes a pilot-controller glossary.

* Available through your local ASA dealer.

DEFENSE MAPPING AGENCY

A free aeronautical chart catalog is available from the Defense Mapping Agency (DMA). It descibes charting publications with coverage beyond the geographic range of NOAA products.

This catalog (please specify DMA Stock No. CATP6V03) may be obtained upon request from the Defense Mapping Agency:

DMA Combat Support Center
ATTN: PMSC
Washington, D.C. 20315-0010
Phone: (301) 227-2495 or
Toll Free: 1-800-826-0342

U.S. GOVERNMENT PRINTING OFFICE

The United States Government Printing Office will provide, free of charge, Subject Bibliographies on a variety of aviation related topics, which will guide you to goverment publications available through the Superintendent of Documents:

○Subject Bibliography No. 13. Aircraft, Airports, and Airways

○Subject Bibliography No. 18. Aviation Information and Training

○Subject Bibliography No. 234. Weather

Order these bibliographies or request a free catalog from:

Superintendent of Documents
U.S. Government Printing Office
Washington, D.C. 20402-9325

Phone: (202) 783-3238 Order and Information Desk

CANADIAN PUBLICATIONS
AERONAUTICAL INFORMATION PUBLICATION (AIP) CANADA

An amendable comprehensive preflight reference manual that provides information concerning rules of the air and procedures for aircraft operations in Canadian airspace.

AIR TOURIST INFORMATION CANADA (Publication TP771E)

This pamplet serves as an initial guide to the pilot planning to fly into Canada. Listed in this publication are the reference documents and charts that are necessary for flight in Canada, along with their contents and price.

FLYING THE ALASKA HIGHWAY IN CANADA (Publication TP2168E)

This free booklet is intended as a guide for the tourist to Canada who intends to fly the Alaska Highway to Alaska. Listed is all Canadian aeronautical information required for flight planning along this route.

These publications and information on other relevant Canadian charts and publications may be obtained from:

Canada Map Office
Energy, Mines and Resources Canada
615 Booth Street
Ottawa, Ontario, Canada K1A ØE9

Phone: (613) 952-7000
FAX: (613) 957-8861

SECTION 3: AERONAUTICAL PLANNING CHART SYMBOLS

GENERAL INFORMATION

Symbols shown are for North Atlantic Route Charts, North Pacific Route Composite and Area Charts. When a symbol is different on any Oceanic Route Chart series it will be annotated NARC NPRC.

VFR WALL PLANNING CHART: Aeronautical Information

AIRPORTS		RADIO AIDS TO NAVIGATION	
AIRPORT DATA	All airports are shown except private or emergency. Selection of airports are made in congested areas based on the following priority: 1. Civil-Military 2. Civil with towers 3. Civil with hard-surfaced runway with services (Attended/Fuel) 4. Civil, unpaved runway with services (Attended/Fuel) 5. Military 6. Civil with hard-surfaced runway no services (Not Attended/No Fuel)	**VHF OMNIDIRECTIONAL RADIO RANGE (VOR)** **DISTANCE MEASURING EQUIPMENT (DME)** **TACTICAL AIR NAVIGATION (TACAN)**	ASP ⬡ VOR Identification —— DCA ⬓ VOR/DME BAL ▽ VORTAC
LANDPLANE-CIVIL Refueling and repair facilities for normal traffic.	◇ BRIDGER MUN		
LANDPLANE CIVIL AND MILITARY Refueling and repair facilities for normal traffic.	◈ CHARLESTON AFB/INTL		
LANDPLANE-MILITARY Refueling and repair facilities for normal traffic.	◉ BERGSTROM AFB		
LANDPLANE LANDING AREA Fuel not available and/or field not attended during normal working hours.	○ BOWERS		

VFR WALL PLANNING CHART: Aeronautical Information

AIRSPACE INFORMATION		NAVIGATIONAL AND PROCEDURAL INFORMATION	
MILITARY REFUELING TRACKS	One Way Two Way	**MAXIMUM ELEVATION FIGURE (MEF)**	(Thousands of Feet) — 6^7 — (Hundreds of Feet) (Highest within each Sectional Chart)
MILITARY TRAINING ROUTES (MTR)	IR307 VR386 VR1531 Four Digits Military Training Routes (MTRs) may extend from the surface upwards. Arrows indicate single direction route. All Military Training Routes (MTRs) (IR and VR) except those VRs at or below 1500' AGL are shown. For altitudes of MTRs, refer to the VFR Wall Planning Chart Tabulation or the DOD Planning AP/1B.	**ISOGONIC LINE AND VALUE** Isogonic lines and values shall be based on the five year epoch chart.	– – 14°E – –
AIR DEFENSE IDENTIFICATION ZONE (ADIZ)	CONTIGUOUS U.S. ADIZ CANADIAN ADIZ Adjoining ADIZ CONTIGUOUS U.S. ADIZ	**TIME ZONE**	Eastern Standard +5=UTC Atlantic Standard +4=UTC All time is Coordinated Universal (Standard) Time (UTC)
SPECIAL USE AIRSPACE Only the airspace effective below 18,000 feet MSL is shown. The type of area shall be spelled out in large areas if space permits.	A-635 P-46 R-6413 W-150 CYD 138 A-Alert Area P-Prohibited Area R-Restricted Area W-Warning Area D – Danger Area (CANADA) ①AREA IDENTIFICATION: In Canada area ident is preceded by the letters CY (CANADA) followed by a number (PROVINCE). QUAIL MOA MOA-Military Operations Area	**INDEX** **Sectional Charts**	WASHINGTON
		NOTE **Warning**	NUMEROUS COASTAL WARNING AREAS REFER TO OPERATIONAL CHART FOR DETAILED INFORMATION

VFR WALL PLANNING CHART: Topographic Information

CULTURE	
POPULATED PLACES OUTLINED	SAVANNAH
Cities and Large Towns	Charleston
Towns and Villages	Conway
BOUNDARIES	
International	– – – – – – –
State	– – – , – – – –

HYDROGRAPHY	
SHORELINES	
MAJOR LAKES AND RIVERS	

RELIEF	
SHADED RELIEF	
SPOT ELEVATIONS	
Position Accurate	• 2216
Position Accurate Elevation Approximate	• 2260±
Critical	• 6973

IFR WALL PLANNING CHART: Aeronautical Information

AIRPORTS	
AIRPORT DATA Civil and private airports are shown having a minimum of 3000' hard-surfaced runway.	Airports/Seaplane Bases shown in Blue have an approved Low Altitude Instrument Approach Procedure published. The DOD FLIP Terminal contains only those shown in DARK BLUE. Airport/Seaplane Bases shown in BROWN do _not_ have a published Instrument Approach Procedure.
LANDPLANE-CIVIL Refueling and repair facilities for normal traffic.	◇　　◇　　◇ Alturas Muni
LANDPLANE CIVIL AND MILITARY Refueling and repair facilities for normal traffic.	◈　　◈　　◈ Charleston AFB/Intl
LANDPLANE-MILITARY Refueling and repair facilities for normal traffic.	◉　　◉　　◉ Biggs AAF
SEAPLANE-CIVIL Refueling and repair facilities for normal traffic.	⬩　　⬩　　⬩ White Mountain Lake
SEAPLANE CIVIL AND MILITARY Refueling and repair facilities for normal traffic.	◈　　◈　　◈ NAS Patuxent River SPB /Trapnell Naples Muni
SEAPLANE-MILITARY Refueling and repair facilities for normal traffic.	◉　　◉　　◉ NAS Corpus Christi SPB

RADIO AIDS TO NAVIGATION	
VHF OMNIDIRECTIONAL RADIO RANGE (VOR) **DISTANCE MEASURING EQUIPMENT (DME)** **TACTICAL AIR NAVIGATION (TACAN)**	ASP ⬡ VOR
	Identification—DCA ⬢ VOR/DME
	BAL ▽ VORTAC
NON-DIRECTIONAL RADIO BEACON (NDB) **MARINE RADIO BEACON (RBn)**	CH ⊚ LF/MF Non-directional Radio Beacon and Identification
	H ⊚ LF/MF Marine Radio Beacon and Identification

IFR WALL PLANNING CHART: Aeronautical Information

AIRSPACE INFORMATION		AIRSPACE INFORMATION	
LOW ALTITUDE AIRWAYS VOR LF/MF Only the controlled airspace effective below 18,000 feet MSL is shown.	V540 — VOR Airway and Identification R6 — LF/MF Airway and Identification Airways with an MEA of 10,000 ft or above (Oxygen may be necessary on extended flights above 10,000 ft MSL)	**MILITARY ROUTES**	┼┼┼┼ ┼┼┼┼ Military IFR ＋＋＋＋ ＋＋＋＋ Military Planning
OCEANIC ROUTES	AR1 — VHF Atlantic Route and Identification AR2 — LF/MF Atlantic Route and Identification	**AIR DEFENSE IDENTIFICATION ZONE (ADIZ)**	CONTIGUOUS U.S. ADIZ CANADIAN ADIZ CONTIGUOUS U.S. ADIZ Adjoining ADIZ
	BR63V — VHF Bahama Route and Identification BR64V BR3L — LF/MF Bahama Route and Identification BR4L	**AIR ROUTE TRAFFIC CONTROL CENTER (ARTCC)**	JACKSONVILLE MIAMI
	A15 ROUTE — LF/MF Oceanic Route and Identification A699 ROUTE	**FLIGHT INFORMATION REGIONS (FIR) and/or (CTA)**	MONTREAL FIR CZUL MONTREAL FIR CZUL Adjoining FIR TORONTO FIR CZYZ CANADIAN ADIZ VANCOUVER FIR CZVR Combined FIR and ADIZ
MILITARY TRAINING ROUTES (MTR)	← IR270 VR371 → Military Training Routes (MTRs) may extend from the surface upwards. Arrows indicate single direction route. All Military Training Routes (MTRs) (IR and VR) except those VRs at or below 1500' AGL are shown. For altitudes of MTRs, refer to the VFR Wall Planning Chart Tabulation or the DOD Planning AP/1B.	**OCEANIC CONTROL AREAS (OCA) and/or (CTA/FIR)**	MIAMI OCEANIC CTA/FIR KZMA NEW YORK OCEANIC CTA/FIR KZNY Adjoining OCA MIAMI OCEANIC CTA/FIR KZMA
		ADDITIONAL OCEANIC CONTROL AREAS	CONTROL 1145 CONTROL 1147

IFR WALL PLANNING CHART: Aeronautical Information

AIRSPACE INFORMATION	
REPORTING POINTS Oceanic only	▲ ▲ Compulsory Bass Shad ——— Name △ △ Non-Compulsory
FACILITY IDENTS	⟨CSV⟩ Facility Ident used with centerline of Oceanic Routes ⟨CSV⟩ and Additional Control Areas
MILEAGES	(200) (200) Total mileage between Radio Aids 20 20 Mileage between Radio Aids, and/or Mileage Breakdown x x Mileage Breakdown All mileages are nautical (NM)
SPECIAL USE AIRSPACE Only the airspace effective below 18,000 feet MSL is shown. The type of area shall be spelled out in large areas if space permits.	A-635 P-56 R-6614 W-64 CYD 147① A-Alert Area P-Prohibited R-Restricted Area W-Warning Area D - Danger Area (CANADA) ① AREA IDENTIFICATION: In Canada area ident is preceded by the letters CY (CANADA) followed by a number (PROVINCE). RUCKER MOA MOA-Military Operations Area

NAVIGATIONAL AND PROCEDURAL INFORMATION	
TIME ZONE	Central Standard +6 = UTC | Eastern Standard +5 = UTC All time is Coordinated Universal (Standard) Time (UTC)
INDEXES **IFR Enroute Low Altitude Charts**	⌐⌐⌐ **L-1** ⌐⌐⌐
Caribbean and S. America Charts	**L-2** C & SA
Canada Charts	**LE-3** CANADA
NOTE	FAA AIR TRAFFIC SERVICE OUTSIDE US AIRSPACE IS PROVIDED IN ACCORDANCE WITH ARTICLE 12 AND ANNEX 11 OF ICAO CONVENTION. ICAO CONVENTION NOT APPLICABLE TO STATE AIRCRAFT BUT COMPLIANCE WITH ICAO STANDARDS AND PRACTICES IS ENCOURAGED.

IFR WALL PLANNING CHART: Topographic Information

CULTURE	
BOUNDARIES **International**	International Boundary (Omitted when coincident ARTCC or FIR) – – – – – – – –
State	– – – – – – – –

HYDROGRAPHY	
SHORELINES	

FLIGHT CASE PLANNING CHART: Aeronautical Information

AIRPORTS

AIRPORT DATA
All civil and private airports are shown having a minimum of 3000' hard-surfaced runway. Selections are made in congested areas.

All airports with a published Low Altitude Instrument Approach Procedure are shown. Civil airports without a published IAP which have a minimum of 3000 feet hard surface runway are also shown. In conjested areas, non-IAP airports are not charted. In Canada and Mexico, airports within 30 nautical miles of the international boundary and/or airways are charted. Airports associated with a radio aid to navigation are also charted. Pvt – Indicates Private use, not available to the general public.

LANDPLANE-CIVIL
Refueling and repair facilities for normal traffic.

◇ Lake City Muni

LANDPLANE CIVIL AND MILITARY
Refueling and repair facilities for normal traffic.

◈ Charleston AFB/Muni

LANDPLANE-MILITARY
Refueling and repair facilities for normal traffic.

⊙ Mac Dill AFB

SEAPLANE-CIVIL
Refueling and repair facilities for normal traffic.

◈ Port Sulphur

PARACHUTE JUMPING AREA

⅄ Refer to Airport/Facility Directory for details

RADIO AIDS TO NAVIGATION

VHF OMNIDIRECTIONAL RADIO RANGE (VOR)
DISTANCE MEASURING EQUIPMENT (DME)
TACTICAL AIR NAVIGATION (TACAN)

ASP ○ VOR

Identification — DCA ▢ VOR/DME

BAL ⬡ VORTAC

NON-DIRECTIONAL RADIO BEACON (NDB)
MARINE RADIO BEACON (RBn)

CH ⊛ LF/MF Non-directional Radio Beacon and Identification

H ⊙ LF/MF Marine Radio Beacon and Identification

FLIGHT SERVICE STATION (FSS)

Name — Macon Co Red underline indicates FSS located at airport site

FLIGHT CASE PLANNING CHART: Aeronautical Information

AIRSPACE INFORMATION		AIRSPACE INFORMATION	
LOW ALTITUDE AIRWAYS VOR LF/MF Only the controlled airspace effective below 18,000 feet MSL is shown.	V249 126 — VOR Airway, Identification and mileage G10 127 — LF/MF Airway, Identification and mileage All mileages are nautical (NM) Airways with an MEA of 10,000 ft or above (Oxygen may be necessary on extended flights above 10,000 ft MSL)	**FLIGHT INFORMATION REGIONS (FIR) and/or (CTA)**	TORONTO FIR CZYZ MONTREAL FIR CZUL TORONTO FIR CZYZ — Adjoining FIR CANADIAN ADIZ VANCOUVER FIR CZVR — Combined FIR and ADIZ
		OCEANIC CONTROL AREAS (OCA) and/or (CTA/FIR)	MIAMI OCEANIC CTA/FIR KZMA NEW YORK OCEANIC CTA/FIR KZNY — Adjoining OCA MIAMI OCEANIC CTA/FIR KZMA
		ADDITIONAL OCEANIC CONTROL AREAS	CONTROL 1419 — Radial or Bearing Line used as centerline for Oceanic Routes and Additional Control Areas ACK — Facility Ident used with centerline of Oceanic Routes and Additional Control Areas
OCEANIC ROUTES	AR-1 — Atlantic Route and Identification BR56V BR66V — VHF Bahama Route and Identification BR1L BR4L — LF/MF Bahama Route and Identification A555 ROUTE G431 ROUTE — LF/MF Oceanic Route and Identification	**REPORTING POINTS** Oceanic only	▲ Compulsory Name —— Champ △ Non-Compulsory
		SPECIAL USE AIRSPACE Only the airspace effective below 18,000 feet MSL is shown. The type of area shall be spelled out in large areas if space permits.	A -690 P-47 R-2604 W-105 CYA 503 ① — A – Alert Area P – Prohibited Area R – Restricted Area W – Warning Area D – Danger Area (CANADA) ① AREA IDENTIFICATION: In Canada area ident is preceded by the letters CY (CANADA) followed by a number (PROVINCE). ENNING MOA — MOA – Military Operations Area
AIR DEFENSE IDENTIFICATION ZONE (ADIZ)	CONTIGUOUS U.S. ADIZ CANADIAN ADIZ CONTIGUOUS U.S. ADIZ — Adjoining ADIZ	**CONTROLLED AIRSPACE**	Class E airspace extends upward from either the surface or a designated altitude to its base of 14,500 ft MSL.

42

FLIGHT CASE PLANNING CHART: Aeronautical Information

NAVIGATIONAL AND PROCEDURAL INFORMATION

MAXIMUM ELEVATION FIGURE (MEF)

(Thousands of Feet) —— **14³** —— (Hundreds of Feet)

(Highest within each Sectional Chart)

TIME ZONE

Pacific Standard
+8=UTC : Mountain Standard
+7 = UTC

All time is Coordinated Universal (Standard) Time (UTC)

INDEXES

Sectional Charts

TWIN CITIES

Canada Charts

GASPE — Designed for visual flights of short duration primarily for pilotage.

Tactical Pilotage Charts

H-23A — Published by Defense Mapping Agency Aerospace Center. Designed for detailed pre-flight planning. Emphasis is on ground features significant in visual and radar low-level high speed navigation.

NAVIGATIONAL AND PROCEDURAL INFORMATION

CLASS B AIRSPACE

Washington

City name in GREEN indicates location is listed on Mileage Table located on back of chart.

Green underline indicates Terminal Area Chart is available

NOTE

FAA AIR TRAFFIC SERVICE OUTSIDE US AIRSPACE IS PROVIDED IN ACCORDANCE WITH ARTICLE 12 AND ANNEX 11 OF ICAO CONVENTION. ICAO CONVENTION NOT APPLICABLE TO STATE AIRCRAFT BUT COMPLIANCE WITH ICAO STANDARDS AND PRACTICES IS ENCOURAGED.

FLIGHT CASE PLANNING CHART: Topographic Information

CULTURE	
POPULATED PLACES Cities and Large Towns	Baltimore — City name in GREEN indicates location is listed on Mileage Table located on back of chart ☐ Wellington
BOUNDARIES International	– – – – – – – International Boundary (Omitted when coincident with FIR)
State	– – – – –

HYDROGRAPHY	
SHORELINES	
MAJOR LAKES AND RIVERS	

RELIEF	
SHADED RELIEF	
SPOT ELEVATIONS Position Accurate Mountain Peaks	2216 ·
Critical	• 6973

43

OCEANIC ROUTE CHARTS: Aeronautical Information

AIRPORTS	
AIRPORT DATA	Airport of Entry (AOE) are shown with four letter ICAO Identifier.
LANDPLANE-CIVIL Refueling and repair facilities for normal traffic.	HONOLULU INTL (PHNL) HONOLULU INTL (PHNL)
LANDPLANE CIVIL AND MILITARY Refueling and repair facilities for normal traffic.	SPOKANE INTL (KGEG) SPOKANE INTL (KGEG)
LANDPLANE MILITARY Refueling and repair facilities for normal traffic.	ELMENDORF AFB (PAED) ELMENDORF AFB (PAED)

RADIO AIDS TO NAVIGATION

		NARC	NPRC
VHF OMNIDIRECTIONAL RADIO RANGE (VOR)	VOR	◉	⬡ ◯
DISTANCE MEASURING EQUIPMENT (DME)	VOR/DME	◉	▢ ▢
TACTICAL AIR NAVIGATION (TACAN)	VORTAC	◉	⬠ ⬠
	TACAN	◉	▽ ▽

NON-DIRECTIONAL RADIO BEACON (NDB) — ◉   ⊙ ⊙ — NARC / NPRC

IDENTIFICATION BOX

Identification — HNL 115.3 / N21°19.7' / W158°01.9' — VHF Frequency / Latitude & Longitude

Identification — NUD 347 / CHAN 77 / N31°52.4' / W176°40.4' — LF/MF Frequency / TACAN Channel / Latitude & Longitude

OCEANIC ROUTE CHARTS: Aeronautical Information

AIRSPACE INFORMATION

AIR TRAFFIC SERVICE (ATS) OCEANIC ROUTES	Identification A50 386 Mileage A50 386 UA23 410 UHF Caribbean Route and Identification All mileages are nautical (NM)
ATS SINGLE DIRECTION ROUTE	B720 B720
AERIAL REFUELING TRACKS	AR-5 17000/FL 300 AR-5 17000/FL 300 One Way Two Way
AIR DEFENSE IDENTIFICATION ZONE (ADIZ)	PHILIPPINE ADIZ PHILIPPINE ADIZ ALASKAN ADIZ ALASKAN ADIZ CANADIAN ADIZ CANADIAN ADIZ
AIR ROUTE TRAFFIC CONTROL CENTER (ARTCC)	SEATTLE (ZSE) SEATTLE (ZSE) OAKLAND (ZOA) OAKLAND (ZOA)

AIRSPACE INFORMATION

FLIGHT INFORMATION REGIONS (FIR) and/or (CTA)	HONOLULU FIR PHZH HONOLULU FIR PHZH HONIARA FIR ANAU HONIARA FIR ANAU NANDI FIR NFFN NANDI FIR NFFN TAIWAN ADIZ MANILA FIR RPMM TAIWAN ADIZ MANILA FIR RPMM
UPPER INFORMATION REGIONS (UIR) UPPER CONTROL AREAS (UTA)	JAKARTA UIR WIIZ JAKARTA UIR WIIZ MERIDA UTA/UIR MMID MERIDA UTA/UIR MMID MAZATLAN UTA/UIR MMZT MAZATLAN UTA/UIR MMZT MEXICO FIR/UIR MMEX FL 450 MEXICO FIR/UIR MMEX FL450
OCEANIC CONTROL AREAS (OCA) and/or (CTA/FIR)	OAKLAND OCEANIC CTA/FIR KZOA OAKLAND OCEANIC CTA/FIR KZOA TOKYO FIR/OCA RJTG TOKYO FIR/OCA RJTG NAHA FIR/OCA RORG NAHA FIR/OCA RORG
ADDITIONAL OCEANIC CONTROL AREAS Note: Limits not shown when coincident with Warning Areas.	CONTROL 1485 CONTROL 1418
BUFFER ZONE	Teeth point to area

45

OCEANIC ROUTE CHARTS: Aeronautical Information

AIRSPACE INFORMATION	
NON-FREE FLYING AREA	Teeth point to area
NORTH ATLANTIC/ MINIMUM NAVIGATION PERFORMANCE SPECIFICATIONS (NAT/MNPS)	NAT/MNPS (FL275 — FL400)
REPORTING POINTS Oceanic only	Name — BORIC ▲ Compulsory ▲ Latitude & Longitude N10.00.0' W162°40.1' △ Non-Compulsory △ BORIC N10°00.0' W162°40.1'
SPECIAL USE AIRSPACE **Warning Area**	W-290 W-186
Special Use	ATLANTIC FLEET WEAPONS RANGE 24A 24B
Flexible Track System	
Free Flow Boundary	
CLASS G AIRSPACE	OPEN AREA CLASS G AIRSPACE

NAVIGATIONAL AND PROCEDURAL INFORMATION	
MILEAGE CIRCLES	300 NM 300 NM All mileages are nautical (NM)
TIME ZONE	−8≡UTC −9≡UTC −8≡UTC −9≡UTC All time is Coordinated Universal (Standard) Time (UTC)
NOTES **Warning**	── WARNING ── AIRCRAFT INFRINGING UPON NON FREE FLYING TERRITORY MAY BE FIRED ON WITHOUT WARNING ── WARNING ── UNLISTED RADIO EMISSIONS FROM THIS AREA MAY CONSTITUTE A NAVIGATION HAZARD OR RESULT IN BORDER OVERFLIGHT UNLESS UNUSUAL PRECAUTION IS EXERCISED ── WARNING ── AIRCRAFT INFRINGING UPON NON FREE FLYING TERRITORY MAY BE FIRED ON WITHOUT WARNING ── WARNING ── UNLISTED RADIO EMISSIONS FROM THIS AREA MAY CONSTITUTE A NAVIGATION HAZARD OR RESULT IN BORDER OVERFLIGHT UNLESS UNUSUAL PRECAUTION IS EXERCISED

OCEANIC ROUTE CHARTS: Aeronautical Information

NAVIGATIONAL AND PROCEDURAL INFORMATION	
COMPASS ROSE	Compass Roses oriented to Magnetic North

NAVIGATIONAL AND PROCEDURAL INFORMATION	
OVERLAP MARKS Area Charts only	NW
PROCEDURAL OPERATIONAL NOTE Central East Pacific (CEP) Routes	CEP COMPOSITE ROUTES FROM FL 290 TO AND INCLUDING FL 450

CEP COMPOSITE ROUTES FROM FL 290 TO AND INCLUDING FL 450

OCEANIC ROUTE CHARTS: Aeronautical Information

CULTURE	
BOUNDARIES **International**	
Convention or Mandate Line	USSR UNITED STATES USSR UNITED STATES
Date Line	MONDAY SUNDAY MONDAY SUNDAY

HYDROGRAPHY	
SHORELINES	

CHARTED VFR FLYWAY PLANNING CHARTS: Aeronautical Information

AIRPORTS	
AIRPORT DATA	No distinction is made between airports with services and those without services. Runways may be exaggerated to clearly portray the pattern. Hard-surfaced runways which are closed but still exist are included in the charted pattern.
LANDPLANES	Rotating Light in operation Sunset to Sunrise DALLAS LOVE (DAL) SKYWAY MANOR (TX1Ø) Paved Runways Unpaved Runways

RADIO AIDS TO NAVIGATION	
VHF OMNIDIRECTIONAL RADIO RANGE (VOR) **DISTANCE MEASURING EQUIPMENT (DME)** **TACTICAL AIR NAVIGATION (TACAN)**	HDF 113.4 VOR FLL 111.4 — Identification / Frequency VOR/DME PBI 115.7 VORTAC
NON-DIRECTIONAL RADIO BEACON (NDB)	PRR 266 Underline indicates no voice on frequency

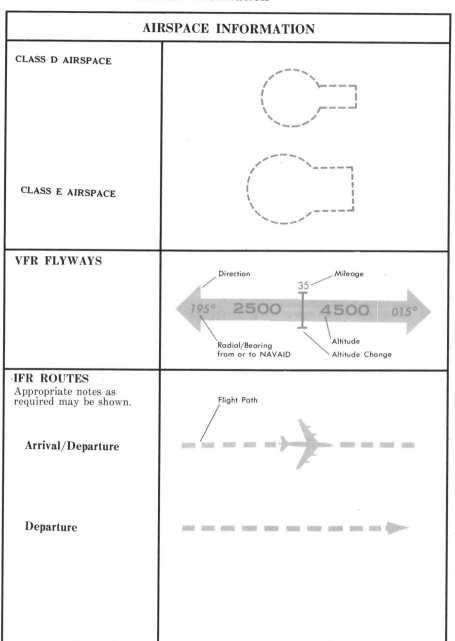

AIRSPACE INFORMATION	
CLASS D AIRSPACE	
CLASS E AIRSPACE	
VFR FLYWAYS	Direction 35 Mileage 195° 2500 4500 015° Radial/Bearing from or to NAVAID Altitude / Altitude Change
IFR ROUTES Appropriate notes as required may be shown. **Arrival/Departure** **Departure**	Flight Path

CHARTED VFR FLYWAY PLANNING CHARTS: Aeronautical Information

AIRSPACE INFORMATION	
MILITARY TRAINING ROUTES (MTR)	IR34 → ← VR1016 Arrows indicate single direction route
SPECIAL USE AIRSPACE Only the airspace effective below 18,000 feet MSL is shown. The type of area shall be spelled out in large areas if space permits.	A-291A TO 2500 —— Altitude (MSL) P-56 R-2916 W-465A A – Alert Area P – Prohibited Area R – Restricted Area W – Warning Area QUAIL MOA TO 2000 MOA – Military Operating Area —— Altitude (MSL)
PARACHUTE JUMPING AREA	
GLIDER OPERATING AREA	
ULTRALIGHT ACTIVITY	

AIRSPACE INFORMATION	
CLASS B AIRSPACE Appropriate notes as required may be shown.	20 NM —— Distance from facility All mileages are nautical (NM) SXC 090° —— Radial from facility All radials are magnetic $\frac{80}{40}$ 80 —— Ceiling of Class B in hundreds of feet MSL 40 —— Floor of Class B in hundreds of feet MSL
MODE C AREA (See FAR 91.215/AIM) Appropriate notes as required may be shown.	MODE C 30 NM Distance from facility All mileages are nautical (NM)
CLASS C AIRSPACE (See FAR 91.215/AIM) Appropriate notes as required may be shown.	$\frac{80}{50}$ 80 —— Ceiling of Class C in hundreds of feet MSL 50 —— Floor of Class C in hundreds of feet MSL
NAVIGATIONAL AND PROCEDURAL INFORMATION **OBSTRUCTIONS** Above Ground Level (AGL) heights are not shown.	629 Less than 1000 ft AGL 808 1808 1808 1000 ft and higher AGL 2049 922 Group Obstruction 2049 974 High Intensity Lights 730 – Elevation of the top Above Mean Sea Level (AMSL) UC – Under contruction or reported: position and elevation unverified. NOTICE: Guy wires may extend outward from structures.
VFR CHECK POINTS	LA PORTE STADIUM Pictorial

CHARTED VFR FLYWAY PLANNING CHARTS: Topographic Information

CULTURE	
RAILROADS	
Single Track	*C & IW*
Multiple Tracks	*SOO LINE*
ROADS	
Dual Lane	FLORIDAS TURNPIKE
Primary	95 40
POPULATED PLACES	
Towns	O LAWRENCEVILLE
BOUNDARIES	
International	— — — — —
POWER TRANSMISSION LINES	
LANDMARKS	■ XEROX

HYDROGRAPHY	
SHORELINES	
MAJOR LAKES AND RIVERS	Bridge
RESERVOIRS	Dam
RELIEF	
SPOT ELEVATIONS Position Accurate Mountain Peaks	4636

SECTION 4: VFR AERONAUTICAL CHART SYMBOLS

GENERAL INFORMATION

Symbols shown are for World Aeronautical Charts, Sectional Aeronautical Charts, and Terminal Area Charts. When a symbol is different on any VFR chart series it will be annotated thus: WAC   or   WAC not shown

CULTURE	
RAILROADS All gauges **Single Track**	
Double Track	
More Than Two Tracks	
Electric	
RAILROADS IN JUXTA-POSITION	
RAILROAD–NON-OPERATING, ABANDONED, DE-STROYED, OR UNDER CONSTRUCTION	
RAILROAD YARDS Limiting Track–To Scale	
Location Only	

CULTURE	
RAILROAD STATIONS	
RAILROAD SIDINGS AND SHORT SPURS	
ROADS Dual Lane Category 1	
Primary Category 2	
Secondary Category 2	
TRAILS Category 3 Provides symbolization for dismantled railroad when combined with label "dismantled railroad."	
ROAD MARKERS U.S. route no. Interstate route no. Air Marked Identification Label	

VFR AERONAUTICAL CHARTS: Topographic Information

CULTURE		CULTURE	
ROAD NAMES	LINCOLN HIGHWAY LINCOLN HIGHWAY ___ WAC	TUNNELS – ROAD AND RAILROAD	
ROADS – UNDER CONSTRUCTION	under construction	FERRIES, FERRY SLIPS AND FORDS	ford ferry ferry ford ferry ferry slip
BRIDGES AND VIADUCTS **Railroad**			
Road			
OVERPASSES AND UNDERPASSES			
CAUSEWAYS		POPULATED PLACES OUTLINED **Large Cities** **Category 1**	

CULTURE	
POPULATED PLACES OUTLINED **Cities and Large Towns** Category 2	 WAC not shown
POPULATED PLACES **Towns and Villages** Category 3	○
PROMINENT FENCES	—×—×—×—×—
BOUNDARIES International	▬▬ ▬▬ ▬▬
State and Provincial	— — — — —
Convention or Mandate Line	— — — — — — — USSR UNITED STATES
Date Line	INTERNATIONAL (Monday) DATE LINE (Sunday)
Time Zone	PST +8 (+7 DT) = UTC MST +7 (+6 DT) = UTC WAC not shown

CULTURE	
MINES AND QUARRIES Shaft Mines and Quarries	⚒
POWER TRANS-MISSION, TELEPHONE & TELEGRAPH LINES	—⊼——————⊼— — -·- - ·- - - - WAC
PIPELINES Underground	———— pipeline ———— — — — underground pipeline — — —
DAMS	
DAM CARRYING ROAD	
PASSABLE LOCKS	locks
SMALL LOCKS	

CULTURE	
WEIRS AND JETTIES	jetties
SEAWALLS	seawall
BREAKWATERS	breakwater breakwater
PIERS, WHARFS, QUAYS, ETC.	piers piers
MISCELLANEOUS CULTURE FEATURES	■ stadium ▣ fort ■ cemetery
OUTDOOR THEATER	

CULTURE	
WELLS Other Than Water	○ oil well
RACE TRACKS	⬯
LOOKOUT TOWERS Air marked identification	◉ P-17 (Site number) 618 (Elevation base of tower)
LANDMARK AREAS	dark area
TANKS	● water ● gas
COAST GUARD STATION	✦ CG
AERIAL CABLEWAYS, CONVEYORS, ETC.	aerial cableway aerial cableway ■—·—·—·—■ ■—·—·—·—■ WAC

HYDROGRAPHY	
SHORELINES **Definite**	
Fluctuating	
Unsurveyed Indefinite	
Man-made	
LAKES Label as required **Perennial** When too numerous to show individual lakes, show representative pattern and descriptive note.	
Non-Perennial (dry, intermittent, etc.) Illustration includes small perennial lake	

HYDROGRAPHY	
RESERVOIRS **Natural Shorelines**	
Man-made Shorelines Label when necessary for clarity	
Too small to show to scale	
Under Construction	
STREAMS **Perennial**	
Non-Perennial	

57

VFR AERONAUTICAL CHARTS: Topographic Information

HYDROGRAPHY	
STREAMS (Continued) **Fanned Out** Alluvial fan	
Braided	
Disappearing	
Seasonally Fluctuating with undefined limits	
with maximum bank limits, prominent and constant	
Sand Deposits In and Along Riverbeds	
WET SAND AREAS Within and adjacent to desert areas	

HYDROGRAPHY	
AQUEDUCTS	aqueduct
Abandoned or Under Construction	abandoned aqueduct
Underground	underground aqueduct
Suspended or Elevated	
Tunnels	
Kanats Underground aqueduct with air vents	underground aqueduct

HYDROGRAPHY	
FLUMES, PENSTOCKS AND SIMILAR FEATURES	_flume_
Elevated	_flume_
Underground	_underground flume_
FALLS	
Double-Line	_falls_
Single-Line	_falls_
RAPIDS	
Double-Line	_rapids_
Single-Line	_rapids_

HYDROGRAPHY	
CANALS	_ERIE_
To Scale	
Abandoned or Under Construction	_abandoned_
To Scale	_abandoned_
SMALL CANALS AND DRAINAGE/IRRIGATION DITCHES **Perennial**	
Non-Perennial	
Abandoned or Ancient	_abandoned_
Numerous Representative pattern and/or descriptive note.	
Numerous	_numerous canals and ditches_

VFR AERONAUTICAL CHARTS: Topographic Information

HYDROGRAPHY	
SALT EVAPORATORS AND SALT PANS MAN EXPLOITED	salt pans
SWAMPS, MARSHES AND BOGS	
HUMMOCKS AND RIDGES	
MANGROVE AND NIPA	mangrove
PEAT BOGS	peat bog
TUNDRA	tundra
CRANBERRY BOGS	cranberry bog

HYDROGRAPHY	
RICE PADDIES Extensive areas indicated by label only.	
LAND SUBJECT TO INUNDATION	
SPRINGS, WELLS AND WATERHOLES	
GLACIERS	
Glacial Moraines	
ICE CLIFFS	
SNOWFIELDS, ICE FIELDS AND ICE CAPS	9000 8000 7000

HYDROGRAPHY	
ICE PEAKS	
FORESHORE FLATS Tidal flats exposed at low tide.	
ROCKS – ISOLATED Bare or Awash	*
WRECKS Exposed	
REEFS – ROCKY OR CORAL	coral
MISCELLANEOUS UNDERWATER FEATURES NOT OTHERWISE SYMBOLIZED	shoals
FISH PONDS AND HATCHERIES	fish hatchery ▪

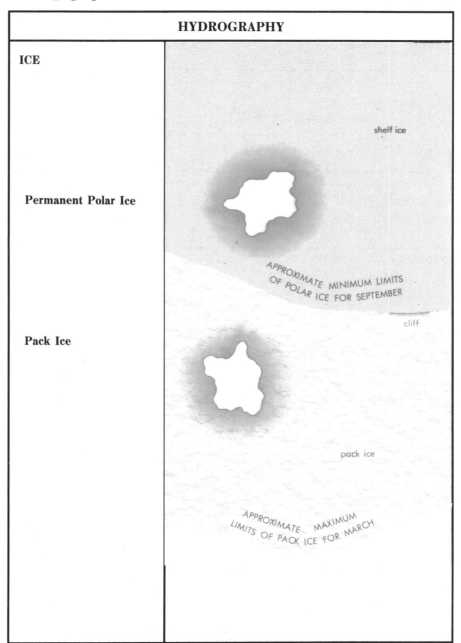

HYDROGRAPHY	
ICE	
Permanent Polar Ice	shelf ice
	APPROXIMATE MINIMUM LIMITS OF POLAR ICE FOR SEPTEMBER
	cliff
Pack Ice	pack ice
	APPROXIMATE MAXIMUM LIMITS OF PACK ICE FOR MARCH

VFR AERONAUTICAL CHARTS: Topographic Information

RELIEF	
CONTOURS Basic	
Approximate	
Intermediate	 WAC
Auxiliary	 WAC
Depression Illustration includes mound within depression	 2000 1000
Values	 5000 6000 5500

RELIEF	
SPOT ELEVATIONS Position Accurate	2216
Position Accurate elevation approximate	2260
Approximate location	2119
Critical	6973
Highest on Chart	12770 WAC 6973
MOUNTAIN PASS	)(12632
HACHURING	

VFR AERONAUTICAL CHARTS: Topographic Information

RELIEF	
UNSURVEYED AREAS Label appropriately as required	UNSURVEYED
DISTORTED SURFACE AREAS	lava
LAVA FLOWS	
SAND OR GRAVEL AREAS	
SAND RIDGES To Scale	
SAND DUNES To Scale	

RELIEF	
SHADED RELIEF	
ROCK STRATA OUTCROP	rock strata
QUARRIES TO SCALE	quarry
STRIPMINES, MINE DUMPS AND TAILINGS To Scale	strip mine mine dump
CRATERS	crater crater
ESCARPMENTS, BLUFFS, CLIFFS, DEPRESSIONS, ETC.	
LEVEES AND ESKERS	levee

VFR AERONAUTICAL CHARTS: Aeronautical Information

AIRPORTS	
LANDPLANE-MILITARY Refueling and repair facilities for normal traffic. All recognizable runways, including some which may be closed, are shown for visual identification. Airports having Airport Traffic Area (CT) are shown in blue, all others in magenta.	PAPAGO AAF 1270 *L 30 NAS MOFFETT CT – 118.3 40 L 92 WAC
SEAPLANE-MILITARY Refueling and repair facilities for normal traffic.	NAS ALAMEDA 00 *L 100 WAC
LANDPLANE-CIVIL Refueling and repair facilities for normal traffic.	SCOTT VALLEY (CA06) 2728 *L 37 122.8 FSS SISKIYOU CO (SIY) 2648 L 75 123.0 SAN FRANCISCO (SFO) INTL CT – 120.5 ATIS 115.8 113.7 12 L 106 123.0 WAC
SEAPLANE-CIVIL Refueling and repair facilities for normal traffic.	ESSEX SKYPARK (28B) 00 L 150 WAC
LANDPLANE CIVIL AND MILITARY Refueling and repair facilities for normal traffic.	SIOUX CITY (SIO) 1097 L 90 123.0 SANTA MONICA (SMO) CT – 120.1 * ATIS 119.15 175 L 82 122.95 WAC

AIRPORTS	
SEAPLANE CIVIL AND MILITARY Refueling and repair facilities for normal traffic.	PORT ARBOUR (ARO) 05 – 150 WAC
LANDPLANE-EMERGENCY No facilities or complete information is not available. Add appropriate notes as required: "closed, approximate position, existence unconfirmed".	ELMA (WA22) 20 L 21 PUBLIC USE – limited attendance or no service available OMH (Pvt) 200 – 17 R RESTRICTED OR PRIVATE – use only in emergency, or by specific authorization AIRPORT - - - UNVERIFIED – a landing area available for public use but warranting more than ordinary precaution due to: U (1) lack of current information on field conditions, and/or (2) available information indicates peculiar operating limitations ABANDONED – depicted for landmark value or to prevent confusion with an adjacent useable landing area. (Normally at least 3000' paved) WAC
SEAPLANE-EMERGENCY No facilities or complete information is not available.	WINTHROP (ME03) 170 – 50 WAC
HELIPORT (Selected)	PENTAGON (ARMY) 995 WAC
ULTRALIGHT FLIGHT PARK (Selected)	F WAC not shown

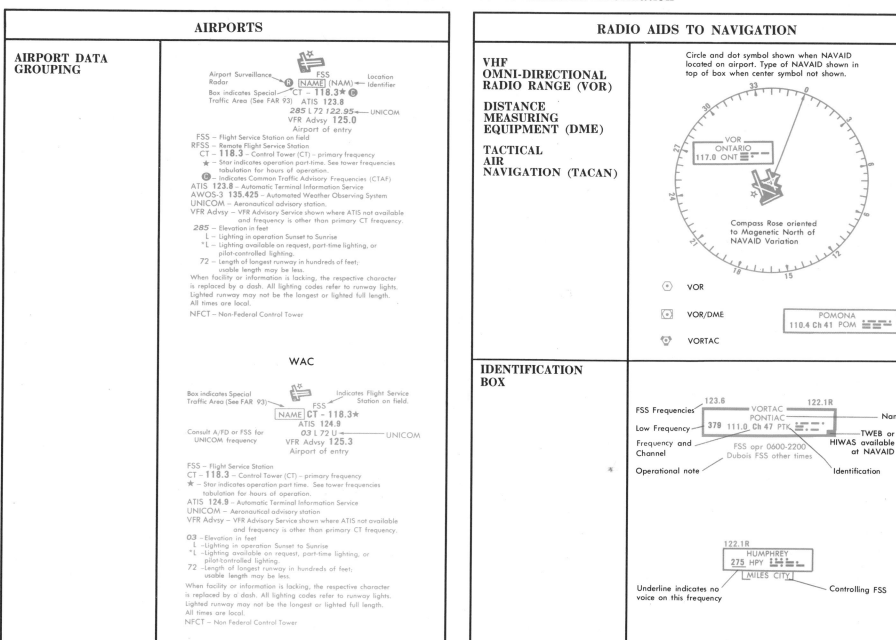

AIRPORTS

AIRPORT DATA GROUPING

Airport Surveillance Radar
Box indicates Special Traffic Area (See FAR 93)
Location Identifier

(R) FSS NAME (NAM)
CT – 118.3★ (C)
ATIS 123.8
285 L 72 122.95 ← UNICOM
VFR Advsy 125.0
Airport of entry

FSS – Flight Service Station on field
RFSS – Remote Flight Service Station
CT – **118.3** – Control Tower (CT) – primary frequency
★ – Star indicates operation part-time. See tower frequencies tabulation for hours of operation.
(C) – Indicates Common Traffic Advisory Frequencies (CTAF)
ATIS **123.8** – Automatic Terminal Information Service
AWOS-3 **135.425** – Automated Weather Observing System
UNICOM – Aeronautical advisory station.
VFR Advsy – VFR Advisory Service shown where ATIS not available and frequency is other than primary CT frequency.
285 – Elevation in feet
L – Lighting in operation Sunset to Sunrise
*L – Lighting available on request, part-time lighting, or pilot-controlled lighting.
72 – Length of longest runway in hundreds of feet; usable length may be less.
When facility or information is lacking, the respective character is replaced by a dash. All lighting codes refer to runway lights. Lighted runway may not be the longest or lighted full length. All times are local.

NFCT – Non-Federal Control Tower

WAC

Box indicates Special Traffic Area (See FAR 93)
Indicates Flight Service Station on field.

NAME CT – 118.3★
ATIS 124.9
Consult A/FD or FSS for UNICOM frequency
03 L 72 U ← UNICOM
VFR Advsy 125.3
Airport of entry

FSS – Flight Service Station
CT – **118.3** – Control Tower (CT) – primary frequency
★ – Star indicates operation part time. See tower frequencies tabulation for hours of operation.
ATIS **124.9** – Automatic Terminal Information Service
UNICOM – Aeronautical advisory station.
VFR Advsy – VFR Advisory Service shown where ATIS not available and frequency is other than primary CT frequency.
03 – Elevation in feet
L – Lighting in operation Sunset to Sunrise
*L – Lighting available on request, part-time lighting, or pilot-controlled lighting.
72 – Length of longest runway in hundreds of feet; usable length may be less.
When facility or information is lacking, the respective character is replaced by a dash. All lighting codes refer to runway lights. Lighted runway may not be the longest or lighted full length. All times are local.

NFCT – Non Federal Control Tower

RADIO AIDS TO NAVIGATION

VHF OMNI-DIRECTIONAL RADIO RANGE (VOR)

DISTANCE MEASURING EQUIPMENT (DME)

TACTICAL AIR NAVIGATION (TACAN)

Circle and dot symbol shown when NAVAID located on airport. Type of NAVAID shown in top of box when center symbol not shown.

VOR
ONTARIO
117.0 ONT

Compass Rose oriented to Magenetic North of NAVAID Variation

VOR

VOR/DME

VORTAC

POMONA
110.4 Ch 41 POM

IDENTIFICATION BOX

FSS Frequencies — 123.6
VORTAC
PONTIAC — Name
122.1R
Low Frequency — 379 111.0 Ch 47 PTK — TWEB or HIWAS available at NAVAID
Frequency and Channel
FSS opr 0600-2200
Dubois FSS other times
Operational note
Identification

122.1R
HUMPHREY
275 HPY
MILES CITY
Underline indicates no voice on this frequency
Controlling FSS

VFR AERONAUTICAL CHARTS: Aeronautical Information

RADIO AIDS TO NAVIGATION

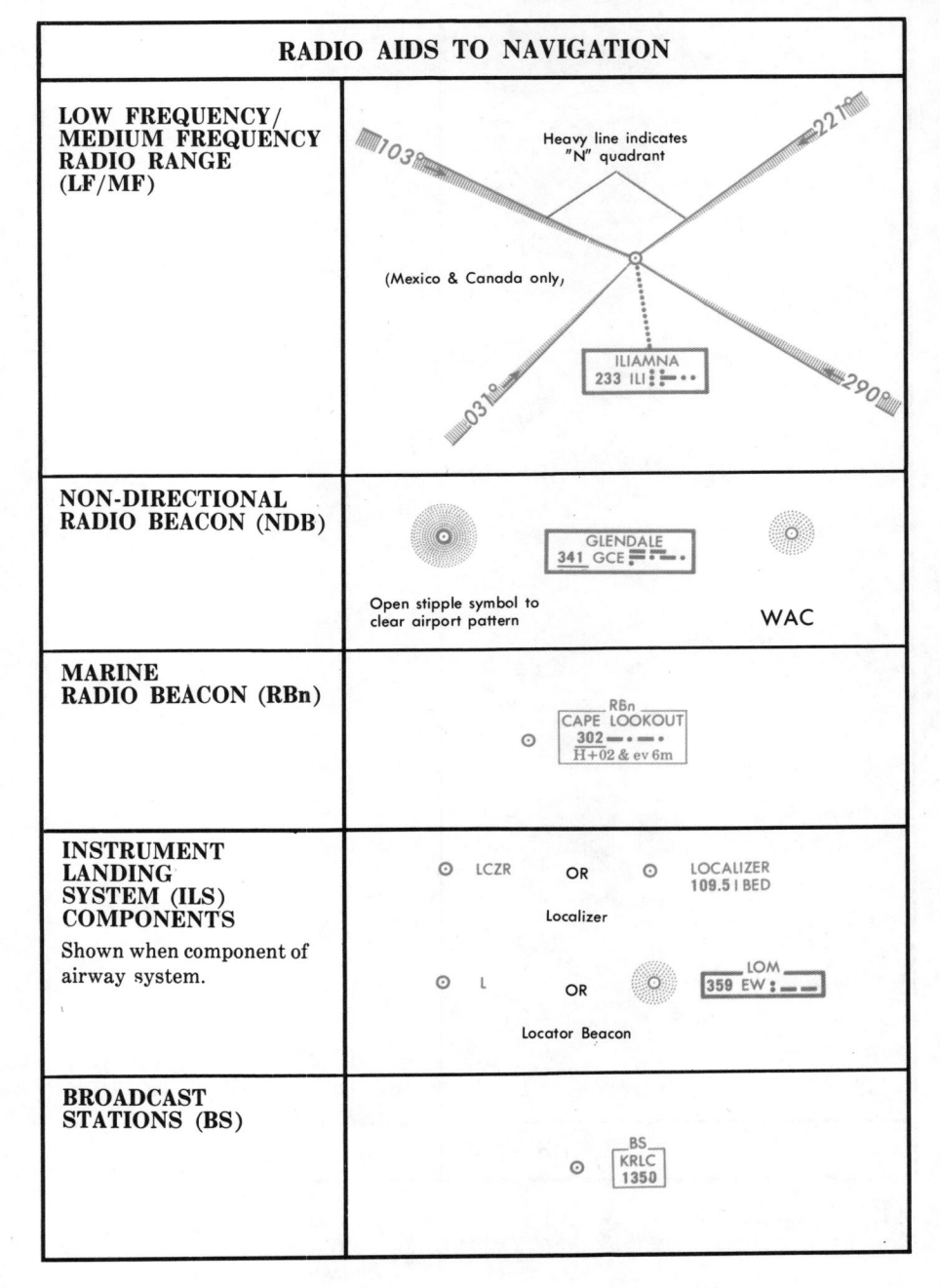

LOW FREQUENCY/ MEDIUM FREQUENCY RADIO RANGE (LF/MF)	Heavy line indicates "N" quadrant (Mexico & Canada only) ILIAMNA 233 ILI
NON-DIRECTIONAL RADIO BEACON (NDB)	GLENDALE 341 GCE Open stipple symbol to clear airport pattern WAC
MARINE RADIO BEACON (RBn)	RBn CAPE LOOKOUT 302 H+02 & ev 6m
INSTRUMENT LANDING SYSTEM (ILS) COMPONENTS Shown when component of airway system.	LCZR OR LOCALIZER 109.5 I BED Localizer L OR LOM 359 EW Locator Beacon
BROADCAST STATIONS (BS)	BS KRLC 1350

RADIO AIDS TO NAVIGATION

FLIGHT SERVICE STATION (FSS)	Heavy line boxes indicate Flight Service Station (FSS). Frequencies 121.5, 122.2, 243.0 and 255.4 are normally available at all FSS's and are not shown above boxes. All other frequencies available at FSS's are shown. Frequencies transmit and receive except those followed by R. R-receive only PONTIAC PTK NO NAVAID of the same name as FSS OR NEEDLES 115.2 Ch 99 EED NAVAID same name as FSS but not an RCO FSS frequencies positioned above thin line NAVAID boxes are remoted to the NAVAID site. Other frequencies at the controlling FSS named are available, however, altitude and terrain may determine their reception. 122.1R FLAGSTAFF 108.2 FLG PRESCOTT — Controlling FSS Thin line box without frequencies and controlling FSS name indicates no FSS frequency available. 122.1 NOGALES RCO TUCSON
REMOTE COMMUNICATIONS OUTLET (RCO)	
AIR FORCE STATION (AFS)	126.2 364.2 AFS CAPE LISBURNE 245 LUR

AIRSPACE INFORMATION	
AIR DEFENSE IDENTIFICATION ZONE (ADIZ) Note: Delimiting line not shown when it coincides with International Boundary, projection lines or other linear features.	CONTIGUOUS U.S. ADIZ
CLASS E AIRSPACE	
CLASS D AIRSPACE	26 Class C Control Zone (Canada)

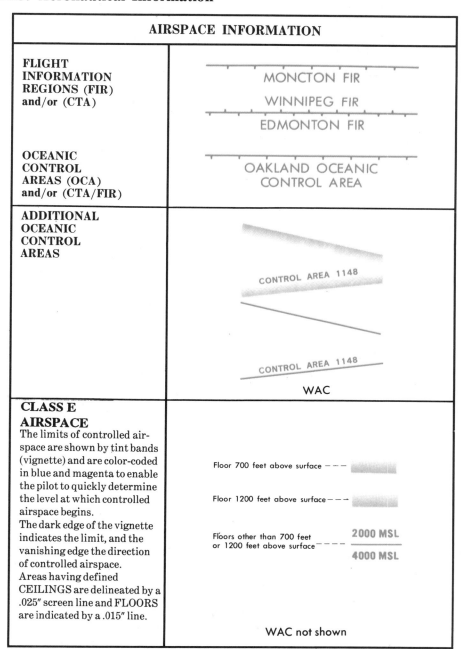

AIRSPACE INFORMATION	
FLIGHT INFORMATION REGIONS (FIR) and/or (CTA) **OCEANIC CONTROL AREAS (OCA) and/or (CTA/FIR)**	MONCTON FIR WINNIPEG FIR EDMONTON FIR OAKLAND OCEANIC CONTROL AREA
ADDITIONAL OCEANIC CONTROL AREAS	CONTROL AREA 1148 CONTROL AREA 1148 WAC
CLASS E AIRSPACE The limits of controlled airspace are shown by tint bands (vignette) and are color-coded in blue and magenta to enable the pilot to quickly determine the level at which controlled airspace begins. The dark edge of the vignette indicates the limit, and the vanishing edge the direction of controlled airspace. Areas having defined CEILINGS are delineated by a .025″ screen line and FLOORS are indicated by a .015″ line.	Floor 700 feet above surface – – – Floor 1200 feet above surface – – ⟶ Floors other than 700 feet or 1200 feet above surface – – – **2000 MSL** / **4000 MSL** WAC not shown

VFR AERONAUTICAL CHARTS: Aeronautical Information

AIRSPACE INFORMATION

LOW ALTITUDE AIRWAYS VOR LF/MF

Low altitude Federal Airways are indicated by center line.

Only the controlled airspace effective below 18,000 feet MSL is shown.

V 2N ← 270°
Alternate Airway Route

255°
V 2
Enroute Airway Route

R 40
LF/MF Airway

B RTE 7
Uncontrolled Route

MILITARY TRAINING ROUTES (MTR)

← IR292

WAC not shown

WARNING, CAUTION NOTES

Used when specific area is not demarcated.

CAUTION: Be prepared for loss of horizontal reference at low altitude over lake during hazy conditions and at night.

FAA urges all pilots operating in the BERING STRAIT area to take utmost precaution to avoid USSR airspace.

WARNING
Aircraft infringing upon Non-Free Flying Territory may be fired on without warning. Consult NOTAMS and Flight Information Publications for the latest air information.

AIRSPACE INFORMATION

SPECIAL USE AIRSPACE

Only the airspace effective below 18,000 feet MSL is shown.

The type of area shall be spelled out in large areas if space permits.

PROHIBITED, RESTRICTED OR WARNING AREA

P-56
OR
R-6401
OR
W-518

ALERT AREA

ALERT AREA
A-631
CONCENTRATED STUDENT
HELICOPTER TRAINING

MILITARY OPERATIONS AREA (MOA)

VANCE 2 MOA

TERMINAL AREA CHART COVERAGE

Sectional only

VFR AERONAUTICAL CHARTS: Aeronautical Information

AIRSPACE INFORMATION

PARACHUTE JUMPING AREA	WAC not shown
HANG GLIDING ACTIVITY	WAC not shown
GLIDER OPERATING AREA	WAC not shown
ULTRALIGHT ACTIVITY	WAC not shown

CLASS B AIRSPACE
Appropriate notes as required may be shown.

LAS VEGAS CLASS B

(Outer limit only shown on WAC)

20 NM – – Distance from facility (TAC)

$\frac{70}{50}$ – – – – Ceiling of Class B in hundreds of feet MSL
– – – – Floor of Class B in hundreds of feet MSL

124.3 – – – ATC Sector Frequency

WAC not shown

CONTACT LAS VEGAS APPROACH CONTROL ON 121.1 OR 257.8 (TAC only)

MODE C AREA
(See FAR 91.215/AIM)
Appropriate notes as required may be shown.

MODE C
30 NM
Distance from facility
All mileages are nautical (NM)

TERMINAL RADAR SERVICE AREA (TRSA)
Appropriate notes as required may be shown.

BILLINGS TRSA

WAC not shown

$\frac{80}{40}$ – – – – Ceiling of TRSA in hundreds of feet MSL
– – – – Floor of TRSA in hundreds of feet MSL

SEE TWR FREQ TAB

WAC not shown

AIRSPACE INFORMATION

AIRSPACE INFORMATION

CLASS C AIRSPACE
(See FAR 91.215/AIM)
Appropriate notes as required may be shown.

48 – – – – Ceiling of Class C in hundreds of feet MSL
30 – – – – Floor of Class C in hundreds of feet MSL
(Outer limit only shown on WAC)

BURBANK CLASS C (WAC only)

SPECIAL AIR TRAFFIC RULES/AIRPORT TRAFFIC AREAS
Appropriate boxed note as required shown adjacent to area.

SPECIAL NOTICE
Pilots are required to obtain an ATC clearance prior to entering this area.

HIGH ENERGY RADIATION AREAS

HAZARDOUS RADAR TRANSMISSIONS SFC TO 4500' MSL

SPECIAL MILITARY ACTIVITY ROUTES

$\frac{90}{20 \text{ AG}}$ ← IR292

$\frac{90}{20 \text{ AG}}$ – – – – Ceiling of MTR in hundreds of feet MSL
– – Floor of MTR in hundreds of feet AGL

SPECIAL MILITARY ACTIVITY CONTACT EDWARDS APPROACH CONTROL ON 127.8 133.65 FOR ACTIVITY STATUS.

WAC not shown

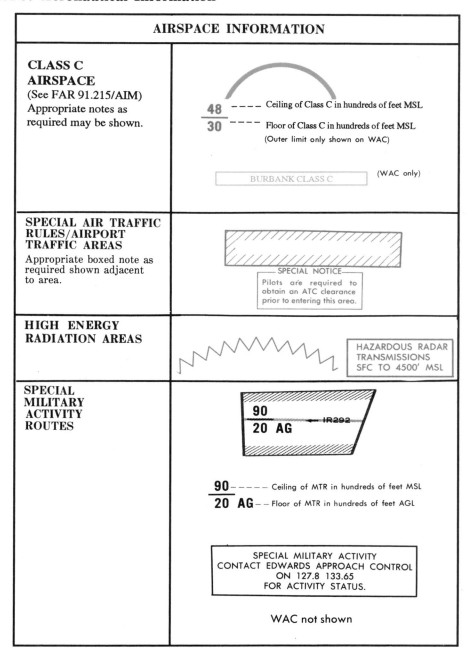

VFR AERONAUTICAL CHARTS: Aeronautical Information

NAVIGATIONAL AND PROCEDURAL INFORMATION	
ISOGONIC LINE & VALUE Isogonic lines and values shall be based on the five year epoch chart.	— 14°E — — — — / — 14°E — — — — WAC
LOCAL MAGNETIC NOTES **Unreliability Notes**	Magnetic disturbances of as much as 78° exists at ground level and 10° or more at 3000 feet above ground level in this vicinity.
COMPASS ROSETTE Shown only in areas void of VOR roses.	

NAVIGATIONAL AND PROCEDURAL INFORMATION	
AERONAUTICAL LIGHTS **Rotating or Oscillating**	Located at aerodrome / In isolated location
Rotating Light with Flashing Code Identification Light	
Rotating Light with Course Lights and Site Number	.5.. / .18.. / 4B..
Flashing Light	Rotating Beacon / Fl

VFR AERONAUTICAL CHARTS: Aeronautical Information

NAVIGATIONAL AND PROCEDURAL INFORMATION

INTERSECTIONS Named intersections used as reporting points. Arrows are directed toward facilities which establish intersection.	CHARL VHF BEACH LF/MF CREST Combined VHF – LF/MF **WAC not shown**
MARINE LIGHTS With Characteristics of Light F–Fixed, Fl–Flashing, Qk–Quick Flashing, I Qk Fl–Interrupted Quick Flashing, Occ– Occulting , Alt–Alternating, Gp–Group, R–Red, W–White, G–Green, B–Blue, (U)–Unwatched, SEC–Sector, Sec–Second. Marine lights are white unless otherwise noted. Alternating lights are red and white unless otherwise noted.	Occ. W R Sector Land light
VISUAL GROUND SIGNS Shore and landmarkers	A33 Arrow points to location of marker M Actual location of ground sign
VFR CHECK POINTS	**GOLDEN GATE BRIDGE** **WAC not shown**

NAVIGATIONAL AND PROCEDURAL INFORMATION

OBSTRUCTION	stack 492 (243) A 675 UC 1959 (1649)	Less than 1000' (AGL) Under Construction 1000' & over (AGL)	stack 502 (417) A 815 UC A 1962 (1676) A **WAC**
GROUP OBSTRUCTION	805 (411) 1887 (1561) 1998 (1704)	Less than 1000' (AGL) 1000' & over (AGL) All in group over 1000' (AGL)	1049 (394) 1921 (1611) 2754 (1986) **WAC**
HI-INTENSITY OBSTRUCTION LIGHTS		Less than 1000' (AGL) 1000' & over (AGL) Group Obstruction	**WAC**
MAXIMUM ELEVATION FIGURE (MEF)	**125**		
SPECIAL CONSERVATION AREAS National Park, Wildlife Refuge, Primitive and Wilderness Areas (As requested by FAA)	HAVASU LAKE NATIONAL WILDLIFE REFUGE **WAC not shown**		

HELICOPTER ROUTE CHARTS: Aeronautical Information

AIRPORTS	
AIRPORT DATA	Only airports/heliports processed through the FAA National Flight Data Center (NFDC) and published in the National Flight Data Digest (NFDD) shall be charted. Other airports that have been requested may be charted as unverified notation. Hard-surfaced runways which are closed but still exist are included in the charted pattern.
LANDPLANES	DU PAGE (DPA) CT – **120.9** ATIS *124.8* 758 L *122.95* Hard-surfaced runways 1500 ft or greater ○ Other than hard-surfaced public use ℞ Private use CONTINENTAL (CON) MILL ROSE **590** FARM (Pvt) **850**
Heliports	Ⓗ Heliports public and private ➕ Trauma Center URSO (Pvt) (Pvt) CONDELL **720** MEMORIAL **720** ⊕ Hospital helipads Ⓗ (Pvt) Helipads located ST THERESE at major airports **700**
Ultralight Flight Park	Ⓕ CLARKE (Pvt) **800**
SEAPLANE	(Pvt) ⚓ MALARD LAKE **800**

AIRPORTS	
AIRPORT DATA GROUPING	Rotating Beacon in operation Sunset to Sunrise Box indicates Special Traffic Area (See FAR 93) → ❘NAME❘ (NAM) ← Location Identifier FSS CT – **118.3**★ Ⓒ ATIS *124.9* 03 L *122.95* ← UNICOM Unverified Heliport → (Unverified) Airport of entry FSS – Flight Service Station on field RFSS – Remote Flight Service Station CT – **118.3** – Control Tower (CT) – primary frequency ★ – Star indicates operation part-time. See tower frequencies tabulation for hours of operation. Ⓒ – Indicates Common Traffic Advisory Frequencies (CTAF) ATIS **124.9** – Automatic Terminal Information Service UNICOM – Aeronautical advisory station. **03** – Elevation in feet L – Lighting in operation Sunset to Sunrise *L – Lighting available on request, part-time lighting, or pilot-controlled lighting. When facility or information is lacking, the respective character is replaced by a dash. All lighting codes refer to runway lights. All times are local. NFCT – Non-Federal Control Tower

HELICOPTER ROUTE CHARTS: Aeronautical Information

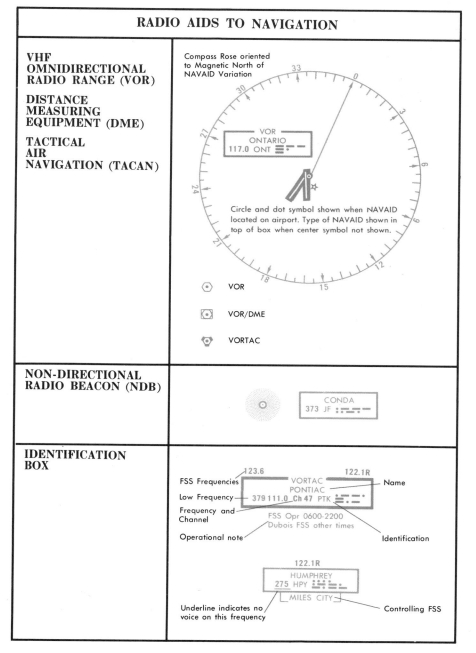

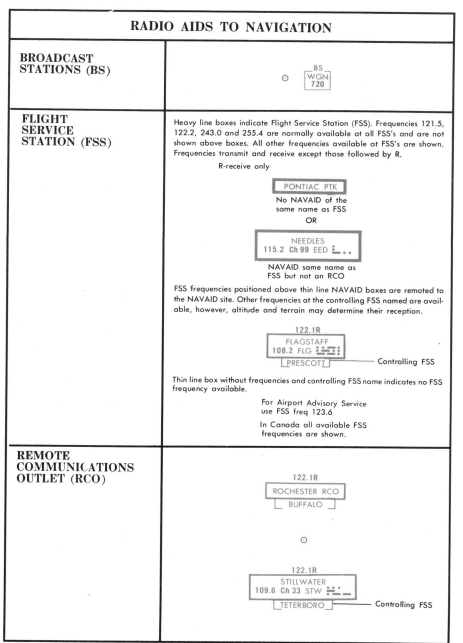

HELICOPTER ROUTE CHARTS: Aeronautical Information

AIRSPACE INFORMATION

CLASS E AIRSPACE

Canada

Class C Control Zone

HELICOPTER ROUTES

Only the controlled airspace effective below 18,000 feet MSL is shown.

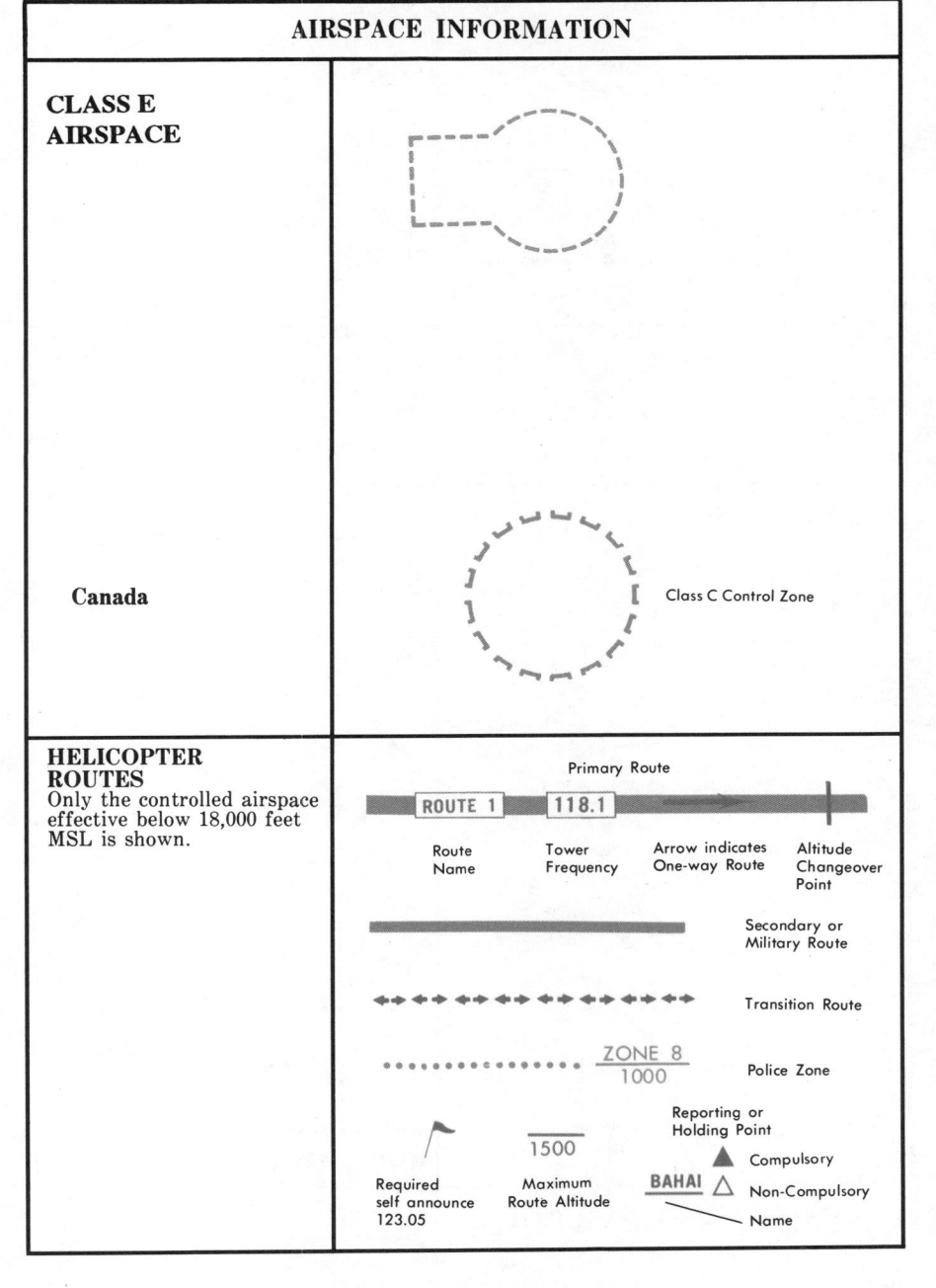

Primary Route

ROUTE 1　118.1

| Route Name | Tower Frequency | Arrow indicates One-way Route | Altitude Changeover Point |

Secondary or Military Route

Transition Route

ZONE 8
1000
Police Zone

1500

Required self announce 123.05

Maximum Route Altitude

BAHAI

Reporting or Holding Point
▲ Compulsory
△ Non-Compulsory
— Name

AIRSPACE INFORMATION

MILITARY TRAINING ROUTES (MTR)

IR203 ▶

◀ VR1064

Arrows indicate single direction route

SPECIAL USE AIRSPACE

Only the airspace effective below 18,000 feet MSL is shown.

The type of area shall be spelled out in large areas if space permits.

A -250　P-73

R-6608　W-290

A – Alert Area
P – Prohibited Area
R – Restricted Area
W – Warning Area

DEMO 2 MOA

MOA – Military Operations Area

SPECIAL AIR TRAFFIC RULES/AIRPORT TRAFFIC AREAS

Appropriate boxed note as required shown adjacent to area.

┌─ SPECIAL NOTICE ─┐
Pilots are required to obtain an ATC clearance prior to entering this area.

WARNING, CAUTION NOTES

Used when specific area is not demarcated.

┌─ WARNING ─┐
Aircraft infringing upon Non-Free Flying Territory may be fired on without warning. Consult NOTAMS and Flight Information Publications for the latest air information.

CAUTION: Be prepared for loss of horizontal reference at low altitude over lake during hazy conditions and at night.

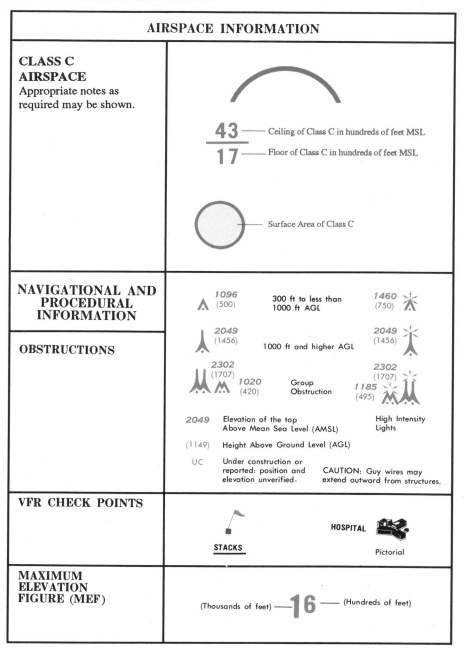

AIRSPACE INFORMATION

PARACHUTE JUMPING AREA	
GLIDER OPERATING AREA	
ULTRALIGHT ACTIVITY	
CLASS B AIRSPACE Appropriate notes as required may be shown.	25 NM — Distance from facility. All mileages are nautical (NM) **70** — Ceiling of Class B in hundreds of feet MSL **15** — Floor of Class B in hundreds of feet MSL Surface Area of Class B CONTROL WASHINGTON APPROACH CONTROL ON 119.85 OR 322.3
MODE C AREA (See FAR 91.215/AIM) Appropriate notes as required may be shown.	MODE C 30 NM Distance from facility. All mileages are nautical (NM)

AIRSPACE INFORMATION

CLASS C AIRSPACE Appropriate notes as required may be shown.	**43** — Ceiling of Class C in hundreds of feet MSL **17** — Floor of Class C in hundreds of feet MSL Surface Area of Class C
NAVIGATIONAL AND PROCEDURAL INFORMATION **OBSTRUCTIONS**	1096 (500) — 300 ft to less than 1000 ft AGL — 1460 (750) 2049 (1456) — 1000 ft and higher AGL — 2049 (1456) 2302 (1707) 1020 (420) — Group Obstruction — 1185 (495) 2302 (1707) 2049 Elevation of the top Above Mean Sea Level (AMSL) — High Intensity Lights (1149) Height Above Ground Level (AGL) UC Under construction or reported: position and elevation unverified. CAUTION: Guy wires may extend outward from structures.
VFR CHECK POINTS	STACKS HOSPITAL Pictorial
MAXIMUM ELEVATION FIGURE (MEF)	(Thousands of feet) — **16** — (Hundreds of feet)

HELICOPTER ROUTE CHARTS: Topographic Information

CULTURE

RAILROADS	
Single Track	BALTIMORE & OHIO
Double Track	SOO LINE

ROADS	
Dual Lane	CENTRAL AVENUE
Primary	495 95 25

BRIDGES	Railroad / Road

POPULATED PLACES OUTLINED	
Large Cities	

BOUNDARIES	
International	
State and Provincial	

CULTURE

POWER TRANSMISSION LINES	

LANDMARKS	Mines and Quarries Race Track Outdoor Theater Tank-water, oil or gas

HYDROGRAPHY

SHORELINES	
MAJOR LAKES AND RIVERS	
RESERVOIRS	Dam

RELIEF

SPOT ELEVATIONS Position Accurate	• 405

SECTION 5: IFR AERONAUTICAL CHART SYMBOLS

IFR ENROUTE LOW ALTITUDE U.S. & ALASKA CHARTS: Aeronautical Information

AIRPORTS	
AIRPORT DATA	Airports/Seaplane Bases shown in BLUE have an approved Low Altitude Instrument Approach Procedure published. Those shown in DARK BLUE have an approved DOD Low Altitude Instrument Approach Procedure and/or DOD RADAR MINIMA published in DOD FLIPS, Alaska Supplement or Alaska Terminal. Airports/Seaplane Bases shown in BROWN do not have a published Instrument Approach Procedure.
LANDPLANE – CIVIL Refueling and repair facilities for normal traffic.	◇ ◇ ◇ Douglas Muni
LANDPLANE CIVIL AND MILITARY Refueling and repair facilities for normal traffic.	◈ ◈ ◉ Charleston AFB/Intl
LANDPLANE– MILITARY Refueling and repair facilities for normal traffic.	◎ ◎ ◎ MCAF Quantico
SEAPLANE–CIVIL Refueling and repair facilities for normal traffic.	⬙ ⬙ ⬙ North Bay
SEAPLANE CIVIL AND MILITARY Refueling and repair facilities for normal traffic.	⬙ ⬙ ⬙ NAS Patuxent River SPB /Trapnell Naples Muni
SEAPLANE– MILITARY Refueling and repair facilities for normal traffic.	⬗ ⬗ ⬗ NAS Corpus Christi SPB
HELIPORT	Ⓗ Ⓗ Ⓗ Allen AHP

AIRPORTS	
AIRPORT DEPICTION	Night Landing Capability: Asterisk indicates lighting on request or operating part of night only. Circle indicates Pilot Controlled Lighting. For information consult the Airport/Facility Directory or FLIP IFR Supplement. Airport Elevation — Name — Longest Landing Runway Length 349 *Ⓛ 80 Automatic Terminal — ASR/PAR Information Service — ATIS *108.5 — Radar Services Availability and Frequency Indicates less than continuous (Name) 185 – 35s No Runway Lighting Capability — Indicates Soft Surface Parentheses around airport name indicate Military Landing Rights not available. Airport elevation given in feet above or below mean sea level. Length of longest runway given to nearest 100 feet with 70 feet as the dividing point (Add 00). Airport symbol may be offset for enroute navigation aids. Pvt – Private use, not available to general public. A box enclosing the airport name indicates FAR 93 Special Requirements – See Directory/Supplement.
AIRPORT RELATED FACILITIES	Pilot to Metro Service (PMSV) ⊶⊷ Continuous Operation ⊶⊸ Less than Continuous ◊ Weather Radar (WXR) ⬦ PMSV and WXR Combined

RADIO AIDS TO NAVIGATION

VHF OMNIDIRECTIONAL RADIO RANGE (VOR) DISTANCE MEASURING EQUIPMENT (DME) TACTICAL AIR NAVIGATION (TACAN)	⬡ VOR ▢ VOR/DME ⬡ VORTAC ▽ TACAN	COMPASS ROSES oriented to Magnetic North of NAVAID which may not be adjusted to the charted Isogonic Values
NON-DIRECTIONAL RADIO BEACON (NDB) MARINE RADIO BEACON (RBn)		LF/MF Non-directional Radio Beacon or Marine Radio Beacon with Magnetic North Indicator UHF Non-directional Radio Beacon LF/MF Non-directional Radio Beacon/DME
INSTRUMENT LANDING SYSTEM (ILS) SIMPLIFIED DIRECTIONAL FACILITY (SDF) LOCALIZER-TYPE DIRECTIONAL AID (LDA)	BACK COURSE ILS Localizer Course with ATC function Feathered side indicates Blue Sector SDF Localizer Course with ATC function LDA	Published ILS and/or Localizer Procedure available Published SDF Procedure available Published LDA Procedure available
COMPASS LOCATOR BEACONS		

RADIO AIDS TO NAVIGATION

BROADCAST STATIONS (BS)	○ WKBW 1520
CONSOLAN STATION	◉
GROUND CONTROL INTERCEPT (GCI)	Ⓖ
WEATHER STATION	○ Norfolk Weather Radio
IDENTIFICATION BOX	

IDENTIFICATION BOX

DME SHUT DOWN
NAME
NAM ⚊ 000.0(T)
DME Chan 00
MN ⚊ 000

VOR with TACAN compatible DME

Overprint of affected data indicates Abnormal Status e.g., SHUT DOWN, MAY BE COMSN, etc.

A solid square indicates weather information available. Enroute weather, when available, is broadcasted on the associated NAVAID frequency. For Terminal weather frequencies see A/G Frequency Tab under associated airport.

(T) Frequency Protection Usable range at 12000'-25 NM.

(Y) Indicates "Y" mode required for reception.

TACAN channels are without voice but are not underlined.

NAME
NAM ⚊ *000
DME Chan 00

NDB with DME

Operates less than continuous or On-Request

Underline indicates No Voice Transmitted on this frequency

IFR ENROUTE LOW ALTITUDE U.S. & ALASKA CHARTS: Aeronautical Information

RADIO AIDS TO NAVIGATION		AIRSPACE INFORMATION	
FLIGHT SERVICE STATION (FSS)	HEAVY LINE BOXES indicate Flight Service Stations (FSS). Frequencies 255.4, 122.2, and emerg. 243.0 and 121.5 are normally available at all FSS's and are not shown above boxes. All other frequencies available at FSS's are shown. Frequencies transmit and receive except those followed by R or T: R — receive only T — transmit only

123.6 122.6 122.1R

Airport Advisory Service (AAS) 123.6

FAYETTEVILLE FYV

Name and identifier for FSS not associated with NAVAID

Frequencies positioned above the thin line NAVAID boxes are remoted to the NAVAID site. Other frequencies at the controlling FSS named are available, however, altitude and terrain may determine their reception.

122.1R

WASHINGTON — Controlling FSS Name

Thin line box, without frequencies and controlling FSS name indicates no FSS frequencies available. | **LOW ALTITUDE AIRWAYS VOR LF/MF**

Only the controlled airspace effective below 18000 feet MSL is shown. | V10 — VOR Airway and Identification

B7 — LF/MF Airway and Identification

B36 — LF/MF Uncontrolled Airway and Identification

B592 / B509 — Air Traffic Service (ATS) Route |
| | | **OCEANIC ROUTES** | AR1 / AR1 — Atlantic Route and Identification

BR 57V — VHF Bahama Route and Identification

BR 1OL — LF/MF Bahama Route and Identification

B112 / A15 ROUTE — Oceanic Route and Identification |
| **AIR GROUND CONTROL** | CTA/FIR NAME — Type of Area Traffic Service FL 180 — Vertical limits of control GND CON 120.5 — A/G Voice call and frequency ACC — Unit providing ATS | **SINGLE DIRECTION ROUTE** | 1000-0600Z — Effective Times of Preferred Route V5 |
| **REMOTE COMMUNICATIONS OUTLET (RCO)** | ○ Flight Service Station (FSS) Remote Communications Outlet (RCO) | **DIRECTION OF FLIGHT INDICATOR** **Canada** | ◄EVEN   ◄EVEN |

IFR ENROUTE LOW ALTITUDE U.S. & ALASKA CHARTS: Aeronautical Information

AIRSPACE INFORMATION		
SUBSTITUTE ROUTE		All relative and supporting data shown in brown See NOTAMs or appropriate publication for specific information
UNUSABLE ROUTE		
MILITARY ROUTES		Military IFR Military Planning
MILITARY TRAINING ROUTES (MTR)	Military Training Routes (MTR's) 5 NM or less IR-107 → VR-134 → Military Training Routes (MTR's) greater than 5 NM IR-113 → VR-133 → Arrow indicates Single Direction Route All MTR's may extend from surface upwards. All MTR's (IR and VR) except those VR's at or below 1500' AGL are shown. CAUTION: Inset charts do not depict Military Training Routes (MTR's).	
ALTIMETER SETTING CHANGE		Altimeter Setting Change when not otherwise defined
AIR DEFENSE IDENTIFICATION ZONE (ADIZ)	CONTIGUOUS U.S. ADIZ ALASKAN ADIZ CANADIAN ADIZ	Adjoining ADIZ

AIRSPACE INFORMATION		
AIR ROUTE TRAFFIC CONTROL CENTER (ARTCC)	NEW YORK WASHINGTON NAME Name 134.3 269.5	ARTCC Remoted Sites with discrete VHF and UHF frequencies
FLIGHT INFORMATION REGIONS (FIR) and/or (CTA)	MONTREAL FIR CZUL MONTREAL FIR CZUL TORONTO FIR CZYZ CANADIAN ADIZ VANCOUVER FIR CZVR	Adjoining FIR Combined FIR and ADIZ
OCEANIC CONTROL AREAS (OCA) and/or (CTA/FIR)	MIAMI OCEANIC CTA/FIR KZMA NEW YORK OCEANIC CTA/FIR KZNY MIAMI OCEANIC CTA/FIR KZMA	Adjoining OCA
ADDITIONAL OCEANIC CONTROL AREAS	CONTROL 1176	
BUFFER ZONE		Teeth point to area
NON FREE FLYING AREA		Teeth point to area

81

IFR ENROUTE LOW ALTITUDE U.S. & ALASKA CHARTS: Aeronautical Information

AIRSPACE INFORMATION		
Fixed-Wing	FSS NO SVFR FREADE (FDE) CT – 126.7 1456 L 110 122.8	Airspace within which fixed-wing special VFR flight is prohibited
Canada	(dashed circle)	Canadian Class "C" Control Zone
	(dotted circle)	Canadian Aerodrome Traffic Zone
REPORTING POINTS	▲ ▲ ALANA ATTIC △ △ ▲ ▲	Compulsory Non-compulsory Off-set arrows indicate facility forming a reporting point (toward LF/MF, away from VHF/UHF)
RADIALS AND BEARINGS	← 217 — — 037 →	Radial Outbound from a VHF/UHF Navigational Aid Bearing Inbound to a LF/MF Navigational Aid
FACILITY IDENTS	DNY 112.1 CA 383	Facility Ident used with radial/bearing lines in the formation of reporting points

AIRSPACE INFORMATION		
DISTANCE MEASURING EQUIPMENT (DME) FIX	→	Denotes DME fix (distance same as airway mileage)
	15 →	DME Radial Line and mileage
TACTICAL AIR NAVIGATION (TACAN) FIX	Ident ——— Chan EDF 84 Radial ——180°/52—— Distance from TACAN from TACAN	
MILEAGES	123 (123)	Total Mileage between Compulsory Reporting Points and/or Radio Aids
	23 23	Mileage between other Reporting Points, Radio Aids, and/or Mileage Breakdown
	x x	Mileage Breakdown
	◄1734►	Overall Mileage (Flight Planning and Military IFR Routes)
	◄1734►	All mileages are nautical (NM)
CHANGEOVER POINT	42 ⌐ 26	VOR Changeover Point giving mileage to Radio Aids (Not shown at midpoint locations)
MINIMUM ENROUTE ALTITUDE (MEA)	3500 V27 6400 → ← 5500 V28	3500 A5 Directional MEA 6400 → ← 5500 G5 All altitudes are MSL unless noted
MINIMUM ENROUTE ALTITUDE (MEA) GAP	V29 MEA GAP	MEA is established with a gap in navigation signal coverage
MAXIMUM AUTHORIZED ALTITUDE (MAA)	MAA-15500 V30	MAA 15500 R5 All altitudes are MSL unless noted

AIRSPACE INFORMATION

MINIMUM OBSTRUCTION CLEARANCE ALTITUDE (MOCA)	MOCA — *2000 4000 V31 *2000 4000 B4
ALTITUDE CHANGE	Change at other than Radio Aids to Navigation
MINIMUM CROSSING ALTITUDE (MCA)	MCA V6 4000 S MCA R6 4000 S
MINIMUM RECEPTION ALTITUDE (MRA)	MRA 9000 R MRA 9000 R
HOLDING PATTERNS	V32 Left Turn V33 Right Turn
AIRWAY RESTRICTION	R-6903 DAYS CHICAGO CENTER/FSS Airway Restriction (Airway penetrates Special Use Airspace) V34

AIRSPACE INFORMATION

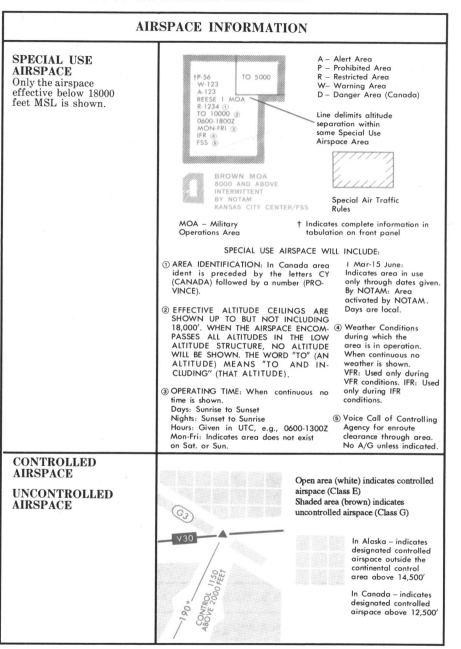

SPECIAL USE AIRSPACE
Only the airspace effective below 18000 feet MSL is shown.

A – Alert Area
P – Prohibited Area
R – Restricted Area
W – Warning Area
D – Danger Area (Canada)

†P-56
W-123
A-123
REESE 1 MOA
R-1234 ①
TO 10000 ②
0600-1800Z
MON-FRI ③
IFR ④
FSS ⑤
TO 5000

Line delimits altitude separation within same Special Use Airspace Area

BROWN MOA
8000 AND ABOVE
INTERMITTENT
BY NOTAM
KANSAS CITY CENTER/FSS

Special Air Traffic Rules

MOA – Military Operations Area

† Indicates complete information in tabulation on front panel

SPECIAL USE AIRSPACE WILL INCLUDE:

① AREA IDENTIFICATION: In Canada area ident is preceded by the letters CY (CANADA) followed by a number (PROVINCE).

② EFFECTIVE ALTITUDE CEILINGS ARE SHOWN UP TO BUT NOT INCLUDING 18,000'. WHEN THE AIRSPACE ENCOMPASSES ALL ALTITUDES IN THE LOW ALTITUDE STRUCTURE, NO ALTITUDE WILL BE SHOWN. THE WORD "TO" (AN ALTITUDE) MEANS "TO AND INCLUDING" (THAT ALTITUDE).

③ OPERATING TIME: When continuous no time is shown.
Days: Sunrise to Sunset
Nights: Sunset to Sunrise
Hours: Given in UTC, e.g., 0600-1300Z
Mon-Fri: Indicates area does not exist on Sat. or Sun.

1 Mar-15 June: Indicates area in use only through dates given. By NOTAM: Area activated by NOTAM. Days are local.

④ Weather Conditions during which the area is in operation. When continuous no weather is shown. VFR: Used only during VFR conditions. IFR: Used only during IFR conditions.

⑤ Voice Call of Controlling Agency for enroute clearance through area. No A/G unless indicated.

CONTROLLED AIRSPACE

UNCONTROLLED AIRSPACE

Open area (white) indicates controlled airspace (Class E)
Shaded area (brown) indicates uncontrolled airspace (Class G)

G3
V30
190°
CONTROL 1150 ABOVE 2000 FEET

In Alaska – indicates designated controlled airspace outside the continental control area above 14,500'

In Canada – indicates designated controlled airspace above 12,500'

IFR ENROUTE LOW ALTITUDE U.S. & ALASKA CHARTS: Aeronautical Information

AIRSPACE INFORMATION

CLASS B AND CLASS C AIRSPACE	CLASS B AIRSPACE RESTRICTIONS TO VFR FLIGHT TO AND INCLUDING 11,000 FEET SEE DENVER VFR TERMINAL AREA CHART OR APPROPRIATE PUBLICATIONS FOR DETAILS
MODE C AREA (See FAR 91.215/AIM)	

NAVIGATIONAL AND PROCEDURAL INFORMATION

ISOGONIC LINE AND VALUE Isogonic lines and values shall be based on the five year epoch chart.	7°E
TIME ZONE	Central Std +6=UTC Eastern Std +5=UTC ‡DURING PERIODS OF DAYLIGHT SAVING TIME (DT) EFFECTIVE HOURS WILL BE ONE HOUR EARLIER THAN SHOWN. ALL STATES OBSERVE DT EXCEPT ARIZONA AND THAT PORTION OF INDIANA IN THE EASTERN TIME ZONE. All time is Coordinated Universal (Standard) Time (UTC)
MORSE CODE	A .— F ..—. K —.— P .——. B —... G ——. L .—.. Q ——.— C —.—. H .... M —— R .—. D —.. I .. N —. S ... E . J .——— O ——— T — U ..— 1 .———— 6 —.... V ...— 2 ..——— 7 ——... W .—— 3 ...—— 8 ———.. X —..— 4 ....— 9 ————. Y —.—— 5 ..... 0 ————— Z ——..

NAVIGATIONAL AND PROCEDURAL INFORMATION

CRUISING ALTITUDES	0° 179°M IFR EVEN Thousands | IFR ODD Thousands VFR or ON TOP EVEN Thousands Plus 500' | VFR or ON TOP ODD Thousands Plus 500' 359°M 180° VFR above 3000' AGL unless otherwise authorized by ATC IFR outside controlled airspace IFR within controlled airspace as assigned by ATC All courses are magnetic
ENLARGEMENT AREA	DETROIT AREA CHART A-1
MATCH MARKS	ALASKA
NOTES	FAA AIR TRAFFIC SERVICE OUTSIDE US AIRSPACE IS PROVIDED IN ACCORDANCE WITH ARTICLE 12 AND ANNEX 11 OF ICAO CONVENTION. ICAO CONVENTION NOT APPLICABLE TO STATE AIRCRAFT BUT COMPLIANCE WITH ICAO STANDARDS AND PRACTICES IS ENCOURAGED.
Warning	WARNING UNLISTED RADIO EMISSIONS FROM THIS AREA MAY CONSTITUTE A NAVIGATION HAZARD OR RESULT IN BORDER OVERFLIGHT UNLESS UNUSUAL PRECAUTION IS EXERCISED.

CULTURE	
BOUNDARIES **International**	— — — — International Boundary (Omitted when coincident with ARTCC or FIR)
Convention or Mandate Line	USSR — — — UNITED STATES
Date Line	INTERNATIONAL DATE LINE MONDAY • SUNDAY

HYDROGRAPHY	
SHORELINES	Water Vignette

IFR ENROUTE HIGH ALTITUDE U.S. & ALASKA CHARTS: Aeronautical Information

AIRPORTS	
AIRPORT DATA	Airports shown have a minimum of 4000' hard-surfaced runway in Alaska and a minimum of 5000' hard-surfaced runway in United States. Airports in BLUE and GREEN have an approved Instrument Approach Procedure published. The DOD FLIP Terminal High Altitude contains only those shown in BLUE.
LANDPLANE-CIVIL Refueling and repair facilities for normal traffic.	◇ ◇ ◇ Baltimore-Washington Intl
LANDPLANE CIVIL AND MILITARY Refueling and repair facilities for normal traffic.	◈ ◈ ◈ Charleston AFB/Intl
LANDPLANE-MILITARY Refueling and repair facilities for normal traffic.	◉ ◉ ◉ Andrews AFB/NAF
MILITARY LANDING RIGHTS	(David Wayne Hooks Mem) Parentheses around airport name indicate Military Landing Rights not available. Applies to U.S. only.

AIRPORTS	
AIRPORT DEPICTION	Airport Elevation — Name — Longest Landing Runway Length, 185 35s, ATIS 120.05 — Automatic Terminal Information Service and Frequency — Indicates Soft Surface — Indicates less than continuous

ALASKA

Airport elevation given in feet above or below mean sea level.

Length of longest runway given to nearest 100 feet with 70 feet as the dividing point (Add 00).

Airport symbol may be offset for enroute navigation aids.

Pvt — Private use, not available to general public. |

RADIO AIDS TO NAVIGATION

RADIO AIDS TO NAVIGATION

VHF OMNIDIRECTIONAL RADIO RANGE (VOR)

DISTANCE MEASURING EQUIPMENT (DME)

TACTICAL AIR NAVIGATION (TACAN)

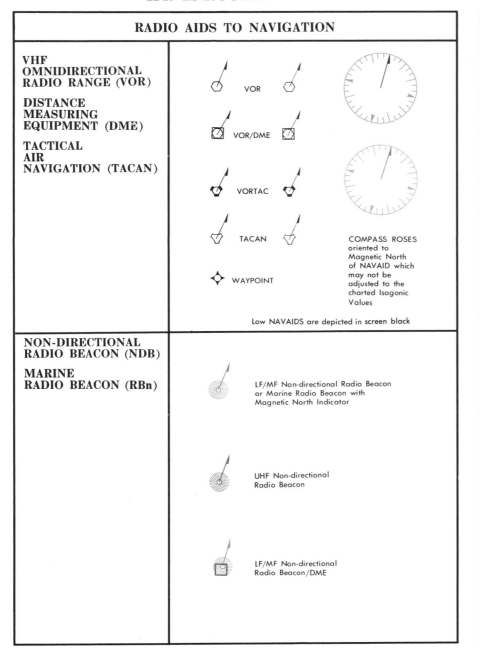

NON-DIRECTIONAL RADIO BEACON (NDB)

MARINE RADIO BEACON (RBn)

IDENTIFICATION BOX

FLIGHT SERVICE STATION (FSS)

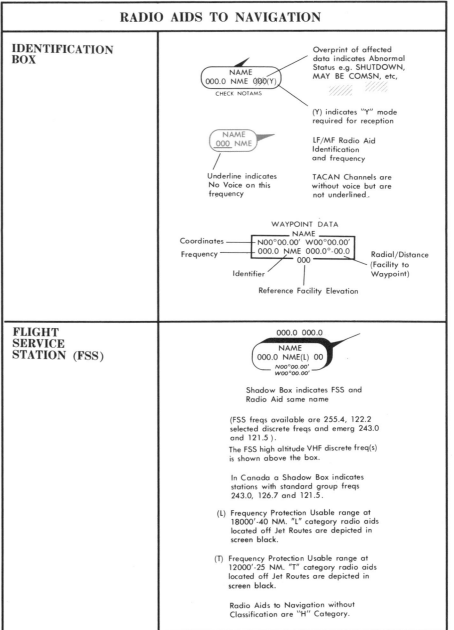

IFR ENROUTE HIGH ALTITUDE U.S. & ALASKA CHARTS: Aeronautical Information

AIRSPACE INFORMATION		AIRSPACE INFORMATION	

HIGH ALTITUDE ROUTES
Only the controlled airspace effective at and above 18,000 feet MSL is shown.

J114 — Jet Route and Identification
J115

J519 — Canadian Jet Route and Identification
J521

J993R — RNAV Route and Identification

R875 — Air Traffic Service (ATS) Route and Identification
R876

OCEANIC ROUTES

AR3 — Atlantic Route and Identification

BR68V — VHF Bahama Route and Identification

BR3L — LF/MF Bahama Route and Identification

A700 — Oceanic Route and Identification
UA301

SINGLE DIRECTION ROUTES
1500-0300Z — Effective Times of Preferred Route
J60
G448 **A312** — Air Traffic Service (ATS) Route

BY PASS ROUTE
Jet Route centerline by-passing a facility which is not part of that specific route

SUBSTITUTE ROUTE
All relative and supporting data shown in brown
(Via or by-passing temporarily shutdown navigational aids)

UNUSABLE ROUTE

MILITARY ROUTE
Military IFR

AIR DEFENSE IDENTIFICATION ZONE (ADIZ)
CONTIGUOUS U.S. ADIZ
ALASKAN ADIZ
CANADIAN ADIZ — Adjoining ADIZ

AIRSPACE INFORMATION	
AIR ROUTE TRAFFIC CONTROL CENTER (ARTCC)	NEW YORK WASHINGTON NAME Name 134.3 269.5 — ARTCC Remoted Sites with discrete VHF and UHF frequencies
FLIGHT INFORMATION REGIONS (FIR) and/or (CTA)	MONTREAL CTA/FIR CZUL MONTREAL CTA/FIR CZUL TORONTO CTA/FIR CZYZ — Adjoining FIR HAVANA CTA/FIR MUHA CUBA ADIZ — Combined FIR and ADIZ
UPPER INFORMATION REGIONS (UIR) UPPER CONTROL AREAS (UTA)	MEXICO UTA/UIR SECTOR 1 MMEX MERIDA UTA/UIR SECTOR 2 MMID MEXICO UTA/UIR SECTOR 3 MMEX — Adjoining UTA/UIR MONTERREY FIR/UIR MMTY — Combined FIR and UIR
OCEANIC CONTROL AREAS (OCA) and/or (CTA/FIR)	HOUSTON OCEANIC CTA/FIR KZHU NEW YORK OCEANIC CTA/FIR KZNY — Adjoining OCA MIAMI OCEANIC CTA/FIR KZMA
ADDITIONAL OCEANIC CONTROL AREAS	NORTH ATLANTIC CONTROL

AIRSPACE INFORMATION	
BUFFER ZONE	Teeth point to area
NON-FREE FLYING AREA	Teeth point to area
REPORTING POINTS	Name — CHAMP N37°31.00' W71°41.00' / TROUT N30°23.00' W77°00.00' — Compulsory; Latitude & Longitude; △ △ Non-Compulsory; Off-set arrows indicate facility forming a reporting point (toward LF/MF, away from VHF/UHF); ◄NR NR► Non-Compulsory Reporting Indicator (No report required at the next compulsory reporting point)
RADIALS AND BEARINGS	◄— 216 — Radial Outbound from a VHF/UHF Navigational Aid; — 036 —► Bearing Inbound to a LF/MF Navigational Aid; ◄—000 000 —► Unusable Radial/Bearing; All radials and bearings are magnetic
FACILITY IDENTS	◄ 115.1 AMG 98; 344 JA ► Facility Ident used with radial/bearing lines in the formation of reporting points

IFR ENROUTE HIGH ALTITUDE U.S. & ALASKA CHARTS: Aeronautical Information

AIRSPACE INFORMATION

DISTANCE MEASURING EQUIPMENT (DME) FIX

← Denotes DME fix (Distance same as route mileage)

⟵50 DME Radial Line and mileage

TACTICAL AIR NAVIGATION (TACAN) FIX

Ident — Chan
EDF 84
Radial from TACAN — 180°/52 — Distance from TACAN

MILEAGES

123 123 Total Mileage between Compulsory Reporting Points and/or Radio Aids

36 36 Mileage between other Reporting Points, Radio Aids, and/or Mileage Breakdown

x x Mileage Breakdown

◄1734► Overall Mileage (Military IFR Routes)
◄1734►

All mileages are nautical (NM)

CHANGEOVER POINT

20
50 VOR Changeover Point giving mileage to Radio Aids (Not shown at midpoint locations)

MINIMUM ENROUTE ALTITUDE (MEA)

J28
MEA-31000 Shown along Routes when other than 18,000'

All altitudes are MSL unless noted

AIRSPACE INFORMATION

MINIMUM ENROUTE ALTITUDE (MEA) GAP

J29 MEA GAP MEA is established with a gap in navigation signal coverage

MAXIMUM AUTHORIZED ALTITUDE (MAA)

MAA-41000
J33 Shown along Routes when other than 45,000'

All altitudes are MSL unless noted

ALTITUDE CHANGE

⊣ ⊢ MEA and/or MAA Change at other than Radio Aids to Navigation
⊣ ⊢

MINIMUM CROSSING ALTITUDE (MCA)

J24 ⊠ J35 ⊠
23000 W 26000 SE

MINIMUM RECEPTION ALTITUDE (MRA)

MRA 8000 ® MRA 9000 ®

HOLDING PATTERNS

△ J30 Left Turn
ATLIC N36°55.05' W75°12.82'

PREPI N39°48.68' W73°15.70'
J31 △ Right Turn

Selected holding reporting points have coordinate values shown

AIRSPACE INFORMATION

SPECIAL USE AIRSPACE
Only the airspace effective at and above 18,000 feet MSL is shown.

The type of area shall be spelled out in large areas if space permits.

```
†P-56
W-123
R-1234 ①
TO 30000 ②
0600-1800Z
MON-FRI ③
IFR ④
ZMA CNTR/FSS ⑤
```

P	– Prohibited Area
R	– Restricted Area
W	– Warning Area
D	– Danger Area (Canada)
A	– Alert Area (Canada)
MFA	– Military Flying Area (Canada)

SPECIAL USE AIRSPACE WILL INCLUDE:

① AREA IDENTIFICATION: In Canada area ident is preceded by the letters CY (CANADA) followed by a number (PROVINCE).

② EFFECTIVE ALTITUDE WHEN CEILING IS NOT UNLIMITED OR FLOOR IS ABOVE 18,000'. THE WORD "TO" (AN ALTITUDE OR FLIGHT LEVEL) MEANS "TO AND INCLUDING" (THAT ALTITUDE OR FLIGHT LEVEL).

③ OPERATING TIME: When continuous no time is shown.
Days: Sunrise to Sunset
Nights: Sunset to Sunrise
Hours: Given in UTC, e.g., 0600-1800Z.
Mon-Fri: Indicates area does not exist on Sat. or Sun.

1 Mar-15 June: Indicates area in use only through dates given.
By NOTAM: Area activated by NOTAM.
Days are Local.

④ Weather Conditions during which the area is in operation. When continuous no weather is shown.
VFR: Used only when VFR Flight can be maintained.
IFR: Used only during IFR Conditions.

⑤ Voice Call of Controlling Agency for enroute clearance through area. No A/G unless indicated.

† Indicates complete information in tabulation on front panel.

CONTROLLED AIRSPACE

Class A Airspace
That airspace from 18,000 feet MSL up to and including FL600, including the airspace overlying the waters within 12 nautical miles of the coast of the 48 contiguous States and Alaska.

AIRSPACE INFORMATION

CONTROLLED AIRSPACE

Canada

SOUTHERN CONTROL AREA

A. ALL FLIGHTS AT OR BELOW FL 600 WILL BE CONDUCTED IN ACCORDANCE WITH THE INSTRUMENT FLIGHT RULES AND, THEREFORE, REQUIRE AN ATC CLEARANCE.

B. "1000 ON TOP" FLIGHTS WILL NOT BE PERMITTED AT OR BELOW FL 600.

C. ALTIMETERS WILL BE SET TO STANDARD PRESSURE (29.92 INS. OF MERCURY OR 1013.2 MBS).

UNCONTROLLED AIRSPACE

Open area (white) indicates controlled airspace
Shaded area (brown) indicates uncontrolled airspace

NAVIGATIONAL AND PROCEDURAL INFORMATION

ISOGONIC LINE AND VALUE
Isogonic lines and values shall be based on the five year epoch chart.

12°W

TIME ZONE

Central Std +6=UTC	Eastern Std +5=UTC

‡ DURING PERIODS OF DAYLIGHT SAVING TIME (DT) EFFECTIVE HOURS WILL BE ONE HOUR EARLIER THAN SHOWN. ALL STATES OBSERVE DT EXCEPT ARIZONA AND THAT PORTION OF INDIANA IN THE EASTERN TIME ZONE.

All time is Coordinated Universal (Standard) Time (UTC)

IFR ENROUTE HIGH ALTITUDE U.S. & ALASKA CHARTS: Aeronautical Information

NAVIGATIONAL AND PROCEDURAL INFORMATION

CRUISING ALTITUDES

18,000' MSL to Flight Level 290

IFR EVEN 2000' Intervals Begin at 18,000' MSL

0° → 179°M

IFR ODD 2000' Intervals Begin at FL 190

VFR or VFR ON TOP EVEN 2000' Intervals Begin at FL 185

359°M — 180°

VFR or VFR ON TOP ODD 2000' Intervals Begin at FL 195

Flight Level 290 and Above

IFR 4000' Intervals Begin at FL 310

0° → 179°M

IFR 4000' Intervals Begin at FL 290

VFR or VFR ON TOP 4000' Intervals Begin at FL 320

359°M — 180°

VFR or VFR ON TOP 4000' Intervals Begin at FL 300

VFR above 3000' AGL
unless otherwise authorized by ATC
IFR Outside controlled airspace
IFR within controlled airspace as assigned by ATC
All courses are magnetic

NO VFR FLIGHTS WITHIN POSITIVE CONTROL AREA

MORSE CODE

A .−	F ..−.	K −.−	P .−−.
B −...	G −−.	L .−..	Q −−.−
C −.−.	H	M −−	R .−.
D −..	I ..	N −.	S ...
E .	J .−−−	O −−−	T −

U ..−	1 .−−−−	6 −....
V ...−	2 ..−−−	7 −−...
W .−−	3 ...−−	8 −−−..
X −..−	4 ....−	9 −−−−.
Y −.−−	5	0 −−−−−
Z −−..		

NAVIGATIONAL AND PROCEDURAL INFORMATION

NOTES

FAA AIR TRAFFIC SERVICE OUTSIDE US AIRSPACE IS PROVIDED IN ACCORDANCE WITH ARTICLE 12 AND ANNEX 11 OF ICAO CONVENTION. ICAO CONVENTION NOT APPLICABLE TO STATE AIRCRAFT BUT COMPLIANCE WITH ICAO STANDARDS AND PRACTICES IS ENCOURAGED.

Warning

— WARNING —
AIRCRAFT INFRINGING UPON NON-FREE FLYING TERRITORY MAY BE FIRED ON WITHOUT WARNING

— WARNING —
UNLISTED RADIO EMISSIONS FROM THIS AREA MAY CONSTITUTE A NAVIGATION HAZARD OR RESULT IN BORDER OVERFLIGHT UNLESS UNUSUAL PRECAUTION IS EXERCISED

Caution

CAUTION: ACCURACY OF AIR TRAFFIC SERVICES RELATIVE TO HAVANA FIR CANNOT BE CONFIRMED. CONSULT NOTAMS

NOTE: AIRCRAFT ENTERING MERIDA UTA/UIR FROM HAVANA CTA/FIR ARE REQUESTED TO CONTACT MERIDA 10 MIN. PRIOR TO BOUNDARY CROSSING ON 128.2

CULTURE	
BOUNDARIES **International**	― ― ― ― International Boundary (Omitted when coincident with ARTCC or FIR)
Convention or Mandate Line	USSR ― ― ― ― ― ― ― UNITED STATES
Date Line	INTERNATIONAL DATE LINE MONDAY • SUNDAY

HYDROGRAPHY	
SHORELINES	Water Vignette

U.S. TERMINAL PROCEDURES PUBLICATION: Aeronautical Information

INSTRUMENT APPROACH PROCEDURE (IAP) CHARTS

88154 Julian Date of Last Revision GENERAL INFORMATION & ABBREVIATIONS

★ Indicates control tower or ATIS operates non-continuously, or non-standard Pilot Controlled Lighting.
  Distances in nautical miles (except visibility in statute miles and Runway Visual Range in hundreds of feet).
  Runway Dimensions in feet. Elevations in feet Mean Sea Level (MSL). Ceilings in feet above airport elevation.
  Radials/bearings/headings/courses are magnetic
# Indicates control tower temporarily closed UFN.

ADF	Automatic Direction Finder
ALS	Approach Light System
ALSF	Approach Light System with Sequenced Flashing Lights
APP CON	Approach Control
ARR	Arrival
ASR/PAR	Published Radar Minimums at this Airport
ATIS	Automatic Terminal Information Service
AWOS	Automated Weather Observing System
AZ	Azimuth
BC	Back Course
C	Circling
CAT	Category
CCW	Counter Clockwise
Chan	Channel
CLNC DEL	Clearance Delivery
CTAF	Common Traffic Advisory Frequency
CW	Clockwise
DH	Decision Heights
DME	Distance Measuring Equipment
DR	Dead Reckoning
ELEV	Elevation
FAF	Final Approach Fix
FM	Fan Marker
GPI	Ground Point of Interception
GS	Glide Slope
HAA	Height Above Airport
HAL	Height Above Landing
HAT	Height Above Touchdown
HIRL	High Intensity Runway Lights
IAF	Initial Approach Fix
ICAO	International Civil Aviation Organization
IM	Inner Marker
Intcp	Intercept
INT	Intersection
LDA	Localizer Type Directional Aid
Ldg	Landing
LDIN	Lead in Light System
LIRL	Low Intensity Runway Lights
LOC	Localizer
LR	Lead Radial. Provides at least 2 NM (Copter 1 NM) of lead to assist in turning onto the intermediate/final course
MALS	Medium Intensity Approach Light System

MALSR	Medium Intensity Approach Light Systems with RAIL
MAP	Missed Approach Point
MDA	Minimum Descent Altitude
MIRL	Medium Intensity Runway Lights
MLS	Microwave Landing System
MM	Middle Marker
NA	Not Authorized
NDB	Non-directional Radio Beacon
NM	Nautical Miles
NoPT	No Procedure Turn Required (Procedure Turn shall not be executed without ATC clearance)
ODALS	Omnidirectional Approach Light System
OM	Outer Marker
R	Radial
RA	Radio Altimeter setting height
Radar Required	Radar vectoring required for this approach
RAIL	Runway Alignment Indicator Lights
RBn	Radio Beacon
RCLS	Runway Centerline Light System
REIL	Runway End Identifier Lights
RNAV	Area Navigation
RPI	Runway Point of Intercept(ion)
RRL	Runway Remaining Lights
Runway Touchdown Zone	First 3000' of Runway
Rwy	Runway
RVR	Runway Visual Range
S	Straight-in
SALS	Short Approach Light System
SSALR	Simplified Short Approach Light System with RAIL
SDF	Simplified Directional Facility
TA	Transition Altitude
TAC	TACAN
TCH	Threshold Crossing Height (height in feet Above Ground Level)
TDZ	Touchdown Zone
TDZE	Touchdown Zone Elevation
TDZ/CL	Touchdown Zone and Runway Centerline Lighting
TDZL	Touchdown Zone Lights
TLv	Transition Level
VASI	Visual Approach Slope Indicator
VDP	Visual Descent Point
WPT	Waypoint (RNAV)
X	Radar Only Frequency

INSTRUMENT APPROACH PROCEDURE (IAP) CHARTS

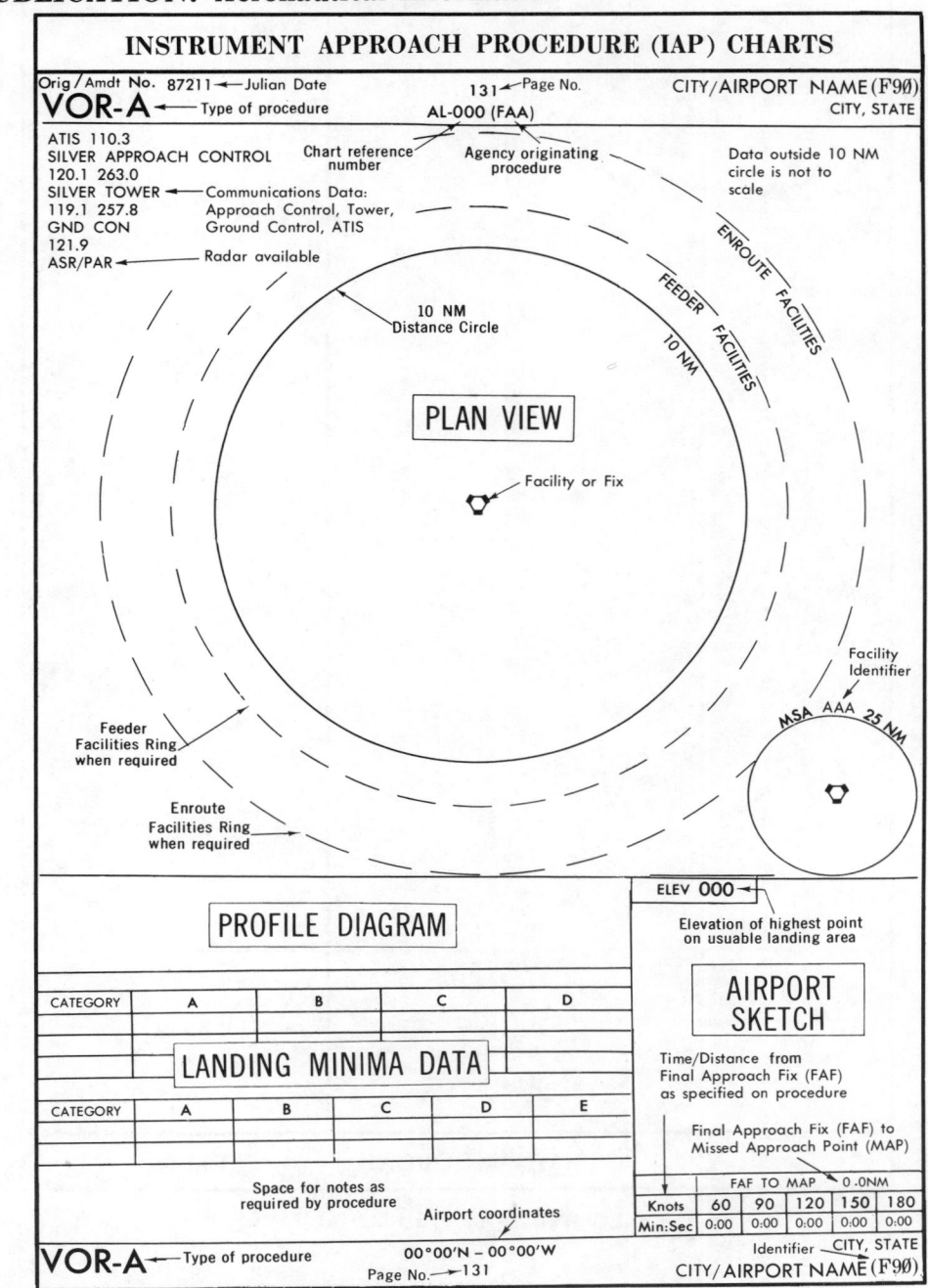

INSTRUMENT APPROACH PROCEDURE (IAP) CHARTS

AIRPORT DIAGRAM/AIRPORT SKETCH

Runways

▬ Hard Surface	▒ Other Than Hard Surface	▒ Overruns, Stopways Taxiways, Parking Areas	⌶ Displaced Threshold
⊠ ⊠ Closed Runways	✕✕✕ Closed Taxiways	⋮⋮⋮ Under Construction	▨ Metal Surface	▬▬ Runway Centerline Lighting

ARRESTING GEAR: Specific arresting gear systems; e.g., BAK-12, MA-1A etc., shown on airport diagrams, not applicable to Civil Pilots. Military Pilots Refer to Appropriate DOD Publications.

⌐ uni-directional ⌐ bi-directional ≷ Jet Barrier

REFERENCE FEATURES

Buildings . . . . ■

Tanks . . . . ●

Obstruction . . . . ⋀

Airport Beacon # . . . . ☆

Runway Radar Reflectors . . . . ⊻

Control Tower # . . . . ▪

Runway length depicted is the physical length of the runway (end-to-end, including displaced thresholds if any) but excluding areas designated as overruns. Where a displaced threshold is shown, an annotation is added to indicate the landing length of the runway; e.g., Rwy 13 ldg 5000'.

Helicopter Alighting Areas Ⓗ ✛ Ⓗ ⚠ ⊞

Negative Symbols used to identify Copter Procedure landing point . . . . Ⓗ ⊞ Ⓗ ⚠ ⊞

Runway TDZ elevation . . . . TDZE 123

Total Runway Gradient . . . . 0.8%→UP

(shown when runway gradient exceeds 0.3%)

⊟ U.S. Navy Optical Landing System (OLS) "OLS" location is shown because of its height of approximately 7 feet and proximity to edge of runway may create on obstruction for some types of aircraft.

Approach light symbols are shown on a separate legend.

Airport diagram scales are variable.

True/Magnetic North orientation may vary from diagram to diagram.

Coordinate values are shown in 1 or ½ minute increments. They are further broken down into 6 second ticks, within each 1 minute increment.

Positional accuracy within ±600 feet unless otherwise noted on the chart.

When Control Tower and Rotating Beacon are co-located, Beacon symbol will be used and further identified as TWR.

NOTE:
Airport diagrams that are referenced to the World Geodetic System (WGS) (noted on appropriate diagram), may not be compatible with local coordinates published in FLIP.

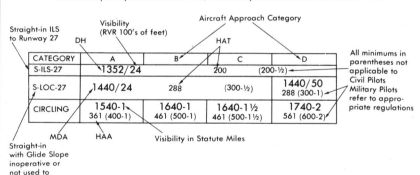

MINIMA DATA

⚠ Alternate Minimums not standard. Civil users refer to tabulation. USA/USN/USAF pilots refer to appropriate regulations.

⚠ NA Alternate minimums are Not Authorized due to unmonitored facility or absence of weather reporting service.

▽ Take-off Minimums not standard and/or Departure Procedures are published. Refer to tabulation.

INSTRUMENT APPROACH PROCEDURE (IAP) CHARTS

AIRCRAFT APPROACH CATEGORIES

Speeds are based on 1.3 times the stall speed in the landing configuration at maximum gross landing weight. An aircraft shall fit in only one category. If it is necessary to maneuver at speeds in excess of the upper limit of a speed range for a category, the minimums for the next higher category should be used. For example, an aircraft which falls in Category A, but is circling to land at a speed in excess of 91 knots, should use the approach Category B minimums when circling to land. See following category limits:

MANEUVERING TABLE

Approach Category	A	B	C	D	E
Speed (Knots)	0-90	91-120	121-140	141-165	Abv 165

LANDING MINIMA FORMAT

In this example airport elevation is 1179, and runway touchdown zone elevation is 1152.

CATEGORY	A	B	C	D
S-ILS-27	1352/24		200	(200-½)
S-LOC-27	1440/24	288	(300-½)	1440/50 288 (300-1)
CIRCLING	1540-1 361 (400-1)	1640-1 461 (500-1)	1640-1½ 461 (500-1½)	1740-2 561 (600-2)

Straight-in ILS to Runway 27 — DH
Visibility (RVR 100's of feet)
Aircraft Approach Category
HAT
All minimums in parentheses not applicable to Civil Pilots Military Pilots refer to appropriate regulations
MDA — HAA — Visibility in Statute Miles
Straight-in with Glide Slope inoperative or not used to Runway 27

RVR/Meteorological Visibility Comparable Values

The following table shall be used for converting RVR to meteorological visibility when RVR is not reported for the runway of intended operation. Adjustment of landing minima may be required – see Inoperative Components Table.

RVR (feet)	Visibility (statute miles)	RVR (feet)	Visibility (statute miles)
1600	¼	4500	⅞
2400	½	5000	1
3200	⅝	6000	1¼
4000	¾		

U.S. TERMINAL PROCEDURES PUBLICATION: Aeronautical Information

INSTRUMENT APPROACH PROCEDURE (IAP) CHARTS

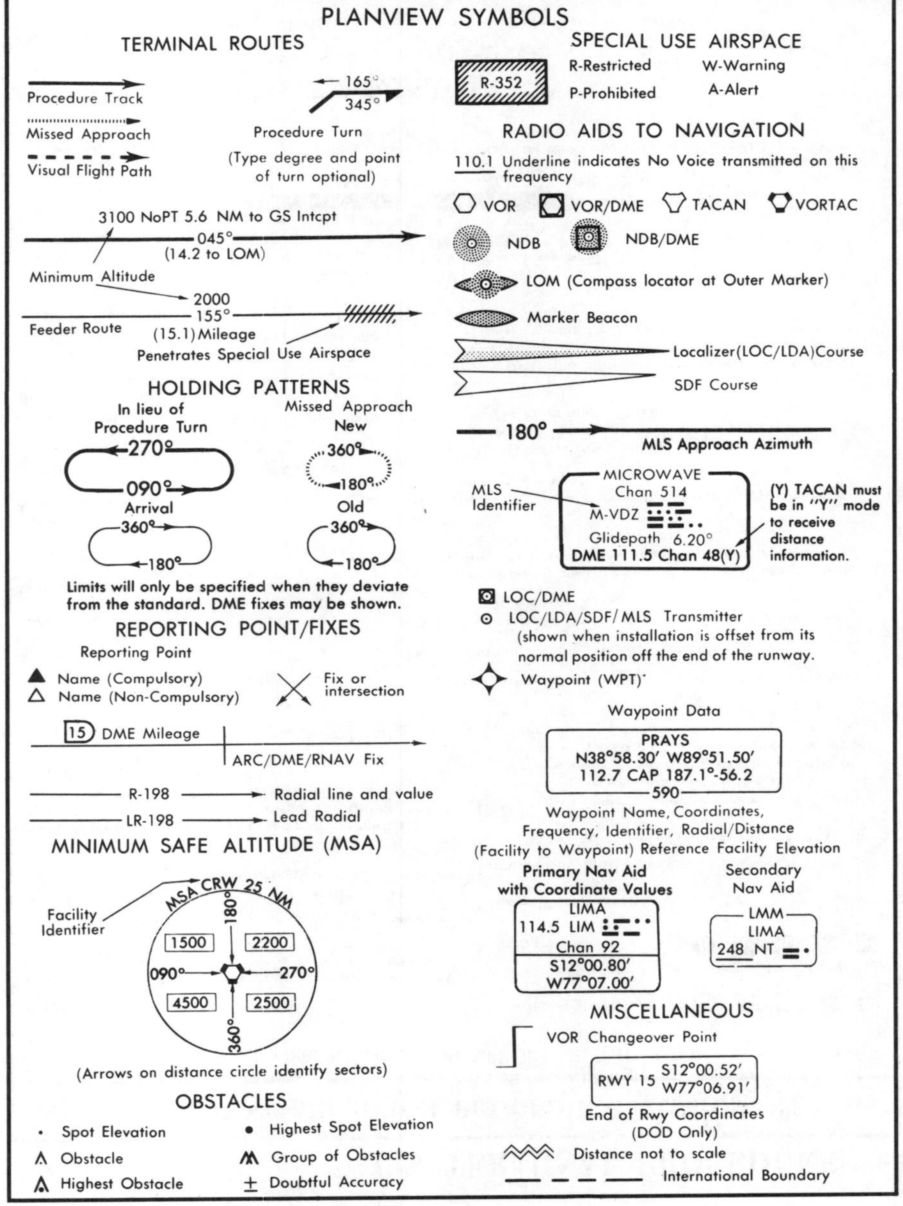

PLANVIEW SYMBOLS

TERMINAL ROUTES

Procedure Track

Missed Approach

Visual Flight Path

— 165°
— 345°
Procedure Turn
(Type degree and point of turn optional)

3100 NoPT 5.6 NM to GS Intcpt
—045°—
(14.2 to LOM)
Minimum Altitude

2000
—155°—
Feeder Route
(15.1) Mileage
Penetrates Special Use Airspace

SPECIAL USE AIRSPACE

R-352

R-Restricted   W-Warning
P-Prohibited   A-Alert

RADIO AIDS TO NAVIGATION

110.1 Underline indicates No Voice transmitted on this frequency

⬡ VOR   ⬡ VOR/DME   ⬡ TACAN   ⬡ VORTAC

NDB   NDB/DME

LOM (Compass locator at Outer Marker)

Marker Beacon

Localizer(LOC/LDA)Course

SDF Course

— 180° —   MLS Approach Azimuth

MLS Identifier

MICROWAVE
Chan 514
M-VDZ
Glidepath 6.20°
DME 111.5 Chan 48(Y)

(Y) TACAN must be in "Y" mode to receive distance information.

⊡ LOC/DME
⊙ LOC/LDA/SDF/MLS Transmitter
(shown when installation is offset from its normal position off the end of the runway.

◆ Waypoint (WPT)

Waypoint Data

PRAYS
N38°58.30' W89°51.50'
112.7 CAP 187.1°-56.2
590

Waypoint Name, Coordinates, Frequency, Identifier, Radial/Distance (Facility to Waypoint) Reference Facility Elevation

Primary Nav Aid with Coordinate Values

LIMA
114.5 LIM
Chan 92
S12°00.80'
W77°07.00'

Secondary Nav Aid

LMM
LIMA
248 NT

HOLDING PATTERNS

In lieu of Procedure Turn
—270°—
—090°—
Arrival
—360°—
—180°—

Missed Approach
New
—360°—
—180°—
Old
—360°—
—180°—

Limits will only be specified when they deviate from the standard. DME fixes may be shown.

REPORTING POINT/FIXES

Reporting Point

▲ Name (Compulsory)
△ Name (Non-Compulsory)

✕ Fix or intersection

15 DME Mileage   ARC/DME/RNAV Fix

— R-198 →   Radial line and value
— LR-198 →   Lead Radial

MINIMUM SAFE ALTITUDE (MSA)

Facility Identifier

MSA CRW 25 NM
180°

1500	2200
090°	270°
4500	2500

360°

(Arrows on distance circle identify sectors)

OBSTACLES

· Spot Elevation
∧ Obstacle
⩕ Highest Obstacle

● Highest Spot Elevation
Ѫ Group of Obstacles
± Doubtful Accuracy

MISCELLANEOUS

VOR Changeover Point

RWY 15 S12°00.52'
W77°06.91'
End of Rwy Coordinates
(DOD Only)

〰〰 Distance not to scale
– – – International Boundary

INSTRUMENT APPROACH PROCEDURE (IAP) CHARTS

PROFILE

—320°—
2400
—125°—
Teardrop Turn
Remain within 10 NM
Procedure Turn
—307°—
2400
—127°—
2156
—GS 3.00°—
—TCH 100—
2400

LOM

Glide Slope Altitude at Outer Marker/FAF
FAF (non-precision approaches)
ILS Glide Slope

Glide Slope
Threshold Crossing Height
Glide Slope Intercept Altitude

Missed Approach Point
Missed Approach Track

Airport Profiles
(Primary)
(Secondary)

DESCENT FROM HOLDING PATTERN

VOR
—127°—
—307°—
1600
1300

VOR
—307°—
—127°—
1600

Final Approach Angle for Vertical Path Computers (RNAV Descent)
—127°—
—3.02°—
MAP WPT

MLS APPROACH

VOR
—360°—
3300
—180°—
MLS 00°R/L
3300
Glidepath 3.0°
TCH 50

M-AJE
6.5
3250
MLS Glidepath
Glidepath Altitude at FAF
Final Approach Fix (FAF)
M-AJE
2.2

FACILITIES/FIXES

FM
IM
MM
NDB
OM
VOR
VORTAC
TACAN
WPT

FIX
INT

ALTITUDES

5500	Mandatory Altitude
2500	Minimum Altitude
4300	Maximum Altitude
3000	Recommended Altitude

PROFILE SYMBOLS

✕ Final Approach Fix (FAF) (for non-precision approaches)

⟋ Glide Slope/Glide Path Intercept Altitude and Final Approach Fix for precision approaches. Unless otherwise indicated the non-precision final approach altitude is to be maintained until the next fix.
2400

2.5 DME Mileage
▼ Visual Descent Point (VDP)
– – → Visual Flight Path

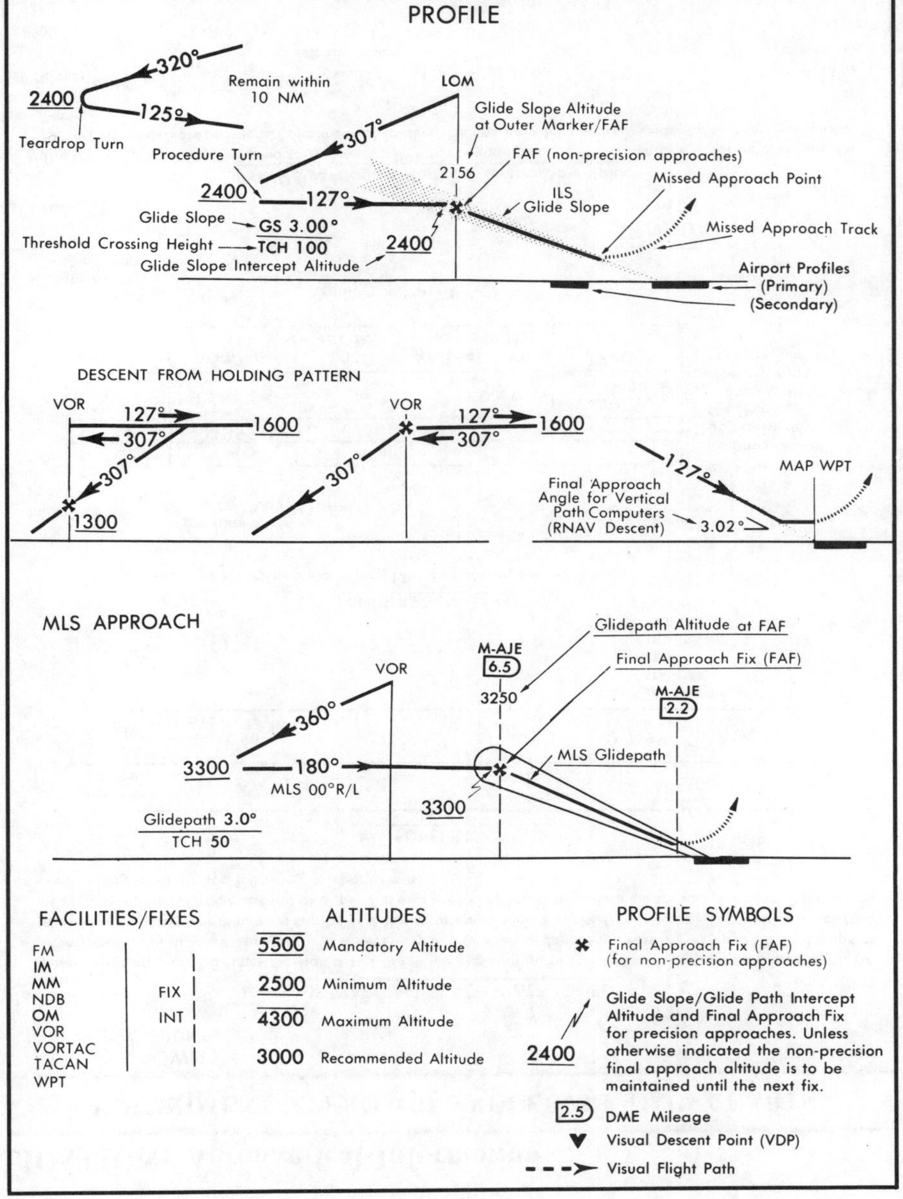

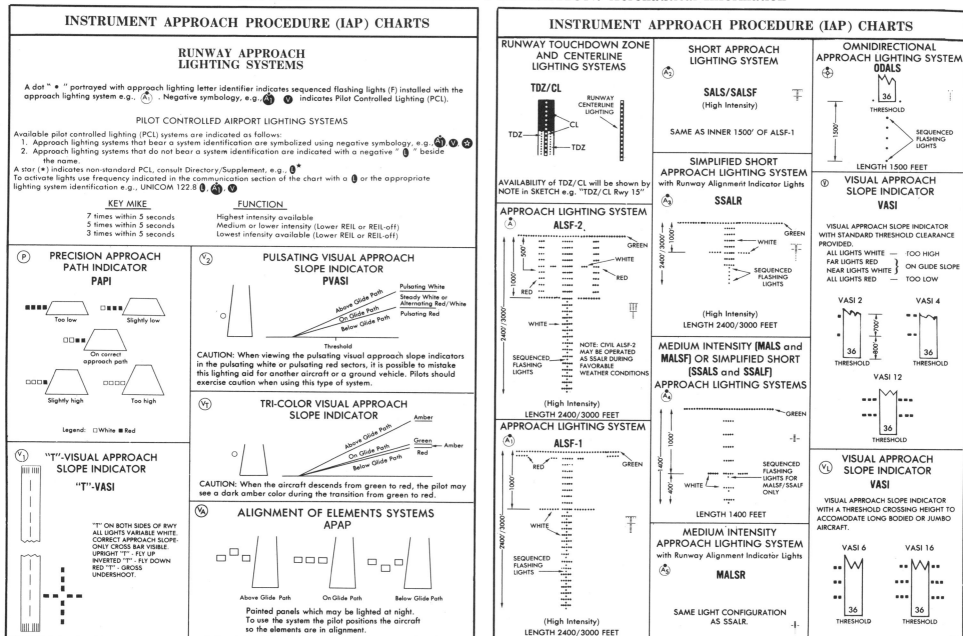

98

U.S. TERMINAL PROCEDURES PUBLICATION: Aeronautical Information

STANDARD TERMINAL ARRIVAL (STAR) CHARTS
STANDARD INSTRUMENT DEPARTURE (SID) CHARTS

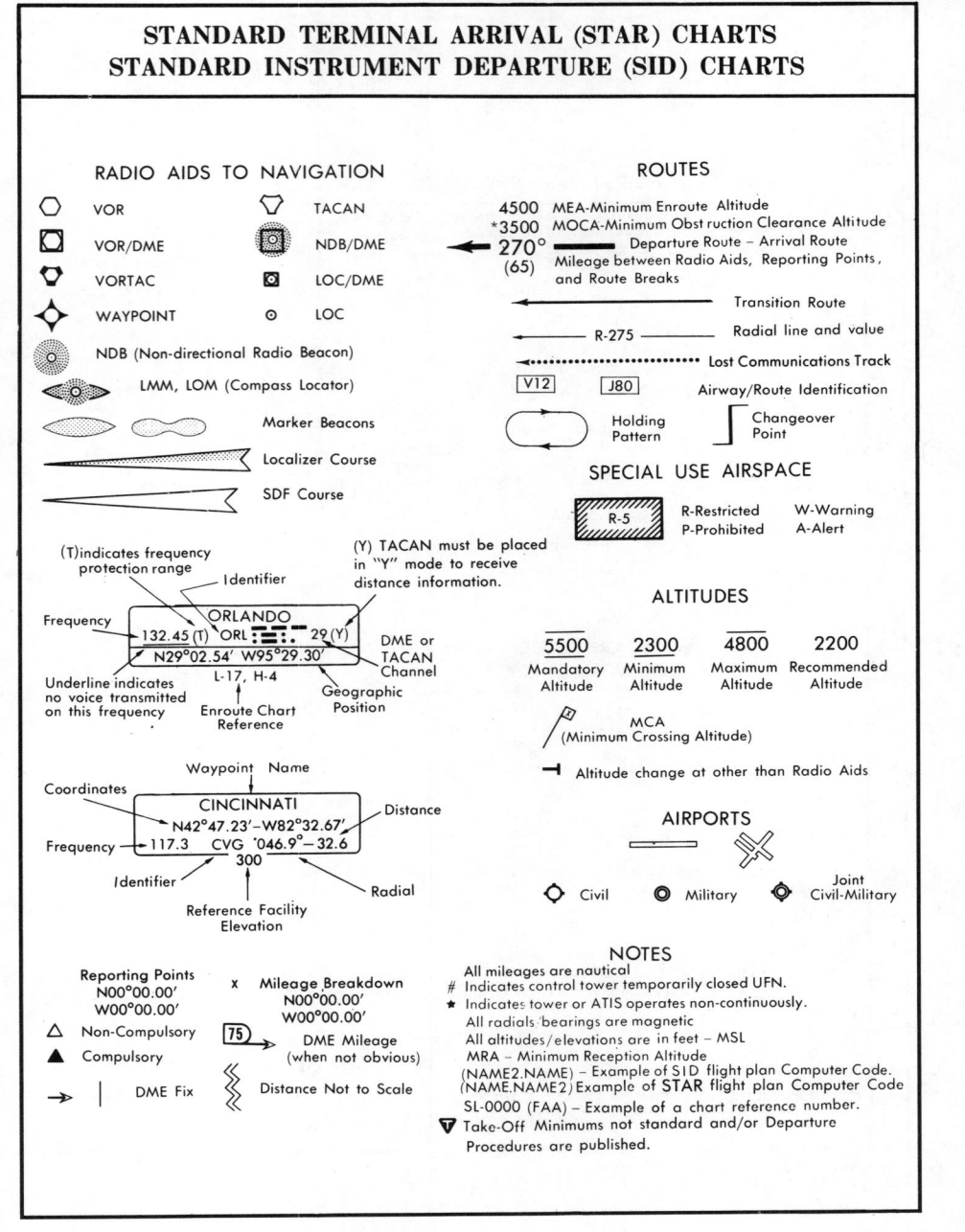

ROUTES

4500 MEA-Minimum Enroute Altitude
*3500 MOCA-Minimum Obstruction Clearance Altitude
270° Departure Route – Arrival Route
(65) Mileage between Radio Aids, Reporting Points, and Route Breaks

Transition Route
R-275 Radial line and value
Lost Communications Track
V12 J80 Airway/Route Identification
Holding Pattern
Changeover Point

SPECIAL USE AIRSPACE

R-5 R-Restricted W-Warning
P-Prohibited A-Alert

ALTITUDES

5500 Mandatory Altitude
2300 Minimum Altitude
4800 Maximum Altitude
2200 Recommended Altitude

MCA (Minimum Crossing Altitude)
Altitude change at other than Radio Aids

AIRPORTS

Civil Military Joint Civil-Military

NOTES

All mileages are nautical
# Indicates control tower temporarily closed UFN.
★ Indicates tower or ATIS operates non-continuously.
All radials/bearings are magnetic
All altitudes/elevations are in feet – MSL
MRA – Minimum Reception Altitude
(NAME2.NAME) – Example of SID flight plan Computer Code.
(NAME.NAME2) Example of STAR flight plan Computer Code
SL-0000 (FAA) – Example of a chart reference number.
▼ Take-Off Minimums not standard and/or Departure Procedures are published.

PROFILE DESCENT PROCEDURE CHARTS

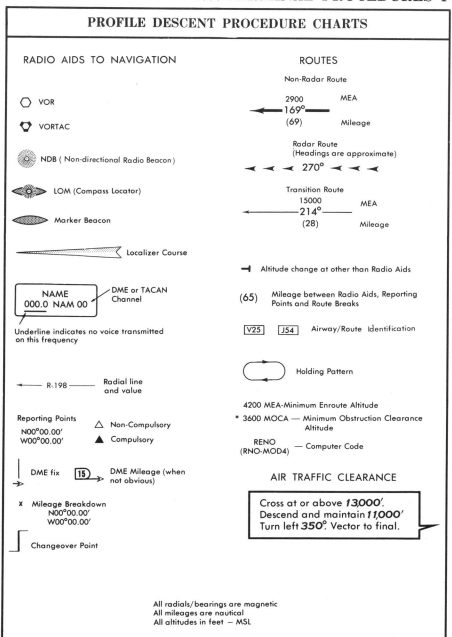

RADIO AIDS TO NAVIGATION

- ⬡ VOR
- ⬡ VORTAC
- ⊙ NDB (Non-directional Radio Beacon)
- ◈ LOM (Compass Locator)
- ◆ Marker Beacon
- ◁ Localizer Course

```
┌─────────────────┐
│      NAME       │──→ DME or TACAN
│  000.0 NAM 00   │    Channel
└─────────────────┘
```
Underline indicates no voice transmitted on this frequency

- ←— R-198 —→ Radial line and value

Reporting Points
N00°00.00'
W00°00.00'
- △ Non-Compulsory
- ▲ Compulsory

- DME fix [15] DME Mileage (when not obvious)

- x Mileage Breakdown
  N00°00.00'
  W00°00.00'

- └ Changeover Point

ROUTES

Non-Radar Route
```
    2900          MEA
←——————169°———
   (69)          Mileage
```

Radar Route
(Headings are approximate)
```
◄  ◄  ◄  270°  ◄  ◄  ◄
```

Transition Route
```
  15000          MEA
←———214°———
  (28)           Mileage
```

- ⊣ Altitude change at other than Radio Aids
- (65) Mileage between Radio Aids, Reporting Points and Route Breaks
- [V25] [J54] Airway/Route Identification
- ⬭ Holding Pattern

4200 MEA-Minimum Enroute Altitude
* 3600 MOCA — Minimum Obstruction Clearance Altitude
RENO
(RNO-MOD4) — Computer Code

AIR TRAFFIC CLEARANCE

Cross at or above *13,000'*.
Descend and maintain *11,000'*
Turn left *350°*. Vector to final.

All radials/bearings are magnetic
All mileages are nautical
All altitudes in feet — MSL

CHARTED VISUAL FLIGHT PROCEDURE (CVFP) CHARTS

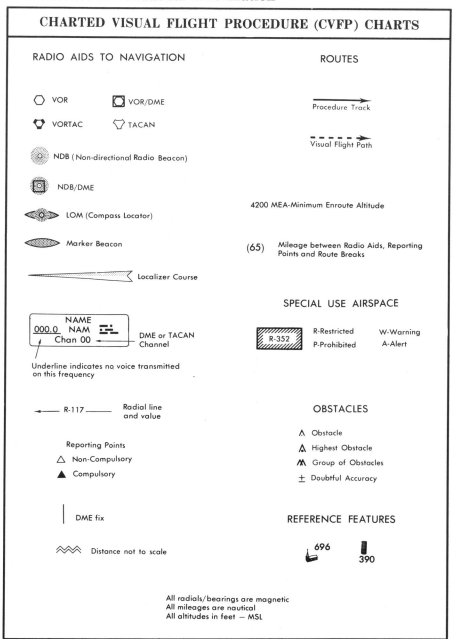

RADIO AIDS TO NAVIGATION

- ⬡ VOR
- ▣ VOR/DME
- ⬡ VORTAC
- ▽ TACAN
- ⊙ NDB (Non-directional Radio Beacon)
- ▣ NDB/DME
- ◈ LOM (Compass Locator)
- ◆ Marker Beacon
- ◁ Localizer Course

```
┌─────────────────┐
│      NAME       │
│ 000.0  NAM  ▪▪  │──→ DME or TACAN
│    Chan 00      │    Channel
└─────────────────┘
```
Underline indicates no voice transmitted on this frequency

- ←— R-117 —— Radial line and value

Reporting Points
- △ Non-Compulsory
- ▲ Compulsory

- DME fix

- ∿∿∿ Distance not to scale

ROUTES

- ——→ Procedure Track
- – – –→ Visual Flight Path

4200 MEA-Minimum Enroute Altitude

- (65) Mileage between Radio Aids, Reporting Points and Route Breaks

SPECIAL USE AIRSPACE

- ▨ R-352
  - R-Restricted
  - P-Prohibited
  - W-Warning
  - A-Alert

OBSTACLES

- Λ Obstacle
- ⋀ Highest Obstacle
- ⋀⋀ Group of Obstacles
- ± Doubtful Accuracy

REFERENCE FEATURES

- 696
- 390

All radials/bearings are magnetic
All mileages are nautical
All altitudes in feet — MSL

U.S. TERMINAL PROCEDURES PUBLICATION: Topographic Information

CULTURE	
BOUNDARIES International	— — – – —

HYDROGRAPHY	
\SHORELINES	
MAJOR LAKES AND RIVERS	

RELIEF	
SPOT ELEVATIONS Position Accurate	2216 .
Highest on Chart	• 6973

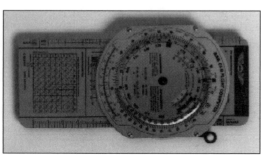

CX-1a Pathfinder

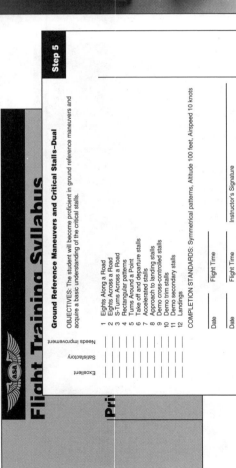

Sample page from the Private Pilot Flight Training Syllabus

Flight Training Syllabus

Step 5

Ground Reference Maneuvers and Critical Stalls–Dual

OBJECTIVES: The student will become proficient in ground reference maneuvers and acquire a basic understanding of the critical stalls.

	Excellent	Satisfactory	Needs Improvement	
1				Eights Along a Road
2				Eights Across a Road
3				S-Turns Across a Road
4				Rectangular patterns
5				Turns Around a Point
6				Take off and departure stalls
7				Accelerated stalls
8				Approach to landing stalls
9				Demo cross-controlled stalls
10				Demo trim stalls
11				Demo secondary stalls
12				Landings

COMPLETION STANDARDS: Symmetrical patterns, Altitude 100 feet, Airspeed 10 knots

Date _____ Flight Time _____
Instructor's Signature _____

Date _____ Flight Time _____
Instructor's Signature _____